More Praise for

A Free Man

"[Sethi] is a smart and wily reporter, a dogged listener, a digger.
. . . Fascinating." —Thomas Larson, *Los Angeles Review of Books*

"Important [and] powerful."—Mridu Rai, *San Francisco Chronicle*

"The experiences of a day laborer are revealed with compassion
and surprising humor by a young Indian journalist."
—Abbe Wright, *O, The Oprah Magazine*

"Vivid and funny narrative nonfiction about an Indian day
laborer—and about the slippery relationship between a journalist
and his subject." —Molly Fischer, *Capital New York*

"[Sethi's] portraits are colorful and sharp, and his descriptions of
various aspects of lower-class Indian culture . . . are unfailingly
lucid." —David Hammerschlag, *Bookslut*

"Incredibly entertaining . . . deftly written. . . . [*A Free Man*] reads
like an adventure." —Subashini Navaratnam, *PopMatters*

"[*A Free Man*] fixes its sights on a single individual: Mohammad
Ashraf is a *mazdoor*—a construction worker—living on the streets
of north Delhi's Sadar Bazaar, forever either recovering from a
hangover or drinking his way into one. . . . Sethi allows Ashraf's
trenchant voice to flood the book, and Ashraf rarely lets him
down." —Samanth Subramanian, *Bookforum*

"A darkly comical and eminently readable work of narrative journalism that brings readers into the heart and soul of old Delhi." —Colleen Mondor, *Booklist*

"A moving and irrepressible work of narrative reporting." —*Publishers Weekly*, starred review

"Alternately sad, defiant, carefree and understated, this journey into a world hidden in plain sight is well worth taking." —*Kirkus Reviews*, starred review

"Funny and disturbing." —Arundhati Roy, author of *The God of Small Things*

"*A Free Man* is a beautiful work of journalism, sympathetic and graceful." —Esther Duflo, author of *Poor Economics* and a MacArthur Fellow

"With *A Free Man*, Aman Sethi comes to the forefront of an extraordinary new generation of Indian nonfiction writers. His compassion and humor are matched by a fierce determination to tell the stories of ordinary Indians, too often forgotten in the scramble for the spoils of the economic boom."—Hari Kunzru, author of *Gods Without Men*

"*A Free Man* is stunning. Not only is Sethi a remarkable reporter and storyteller, but he possesses a novelist's ear for language, sense of the absurd, and perfect pitch. I'm bowled over, totally." —Sylvia Nasar, author of *A Beautiful Mind* and *A Grand Pursuit*

"Funny, poignant, and deeply moving, *A Free Man* is an extraordinary vignette into an extraordinary life." —Siddhartha Mukherjee, author of *The Emperor of All Maladies*

A
FREE
MAN

AMAN SETHI

W. W. Norton & Company
New York • London

For information about permission to reproduce selections from this book,
write to Permissions, W. W. Norton & Company, Inc., 500 Fifth Avenue,
New York, NY 10110

For information about special discounts for bulk purchases, please contact
W. W. Norton Special Sales at specialsales@wwnorton.com or 800-233-4830

Manufacturing by RR Donnelley, Harrisonburg
Production manager: Devon Zahn

Library of Congress Cataloging-in-Publication Data

Sethi, Aman, 1983–
A free man : a true story of life and death in Delhi / Aman Sethi. —
1st American ed.
p. cm.
ISBN 978-0-393-08890-8 (hardcover)
1. Mohammed, Ashraf, 1966– 2. Homeless persons—India—Delhi—Biography.
3. Day laborers—India—Delhi—Biography. 4. Delhi (India)—Biography. 5. Life
change events—India—Delhi—Case studies. 6. Delhi (India)—Social conditions.
7. Urban poor—India—Delhi. 8. Marginality, Social—India—Delhi. I. Title.
HV4600.D4S48 2012
362.5'92092—dc23
[B]
2012022384

ISBN 978-0-393-34660-2 pbk.

W. W. Norton & Company, Inc.
500 Fifth Avenue, New York, N.Y. 10110
www.wwnorton.com

W. W. Norton & Company Ltd.
Castle House, 75/76 Wells Street, London W1T 3QT

1 2 3 4 5 6 7 8 9 0

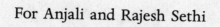

For Anjali and Rajesh Sethi

one

AZADI,

or Freedom

1

'At forty,' says Mohammed Ashraf, delicately picking at the joint's smouldering cherry, 'a man starts to fear strangers.'

'Accha?'

'At twenty, he is cautious; at thirty he is wary, suspicious by thirty-five, but fear? Fear starts at forty.'

'Accha bhai, now pass.'

Mohammed Ashraf looks up with an air of enquiry in his bloodshot eyes. Our circle of huddled figures stares back hungrily. He takes another hit from the joint. 'At forty his arms weaken. His shoulders sag a bit, his moustache droops. His voice might crack—like a phata hua harmonium. His friends, if he still has any...'

'Pass, Ashraf bhai. Pass.' Muffled, yet insistent, a voice has emerged from somewhere in our midst. For a quarter of an hour we have sat in silence as Ashraf has extolled the virtues of ticketless train travel, counted the blessings of being in jail, and, with a rolled-up shirt in one hand and a slender paintbrush in the other, demonstrated the proper technique for skinning chicken. We have stifled our yawns, crossed and uncrossed our legs, and swatted away squadrons of mosquitoes as Ashraf has pulled and sucked and ashed at the joint wedged firmly between his fingers.

'Sorry, does someone want this?'

The crowd shuffles. In our circle, the joint has moderated conversation; microphone-like, it singles out its holder as the speaker. Tranquillized by the ganja, exhausted by a long day of work, Ashraf is nonetheless invigorated by the ease with which he has commanded the undivided attention of all present. We've stared fixedly as he's brought the joint to his lips and taken deep, satisfying drags; we've inhaled as he's inhaled, winced as he's choked on the sharp, bitter smoke; we've held our breath to allow the weed to exert its mystical powers, and exhaled as he's expelled smoke from his lungs.

'Arre, pass, Ashraf bhai?' Rehaan asks again. They look at each other for the briefest of instants, wondering if the impoliteness of hurrying someone's hit is outweighed by that of holding the joint too long. Ashraf knows that he can hold off passing the joint for only as long as he can keep us immersed in his tale, and we have finally run out of patience. It was an interesting story, but a timer has finally gone off in someone's head. I can hear it; it sounds like the tapping of a screwdriver against an empty tea glass. It's Lalloo.

Lalloo has finished his whisky, Rehaan has smoked his beedi down to his fingertips, and I? I have maintained a firm grip on the edge of the concrete stair, and am happy to report that I haven't fallen over.

The joint has passed on: Rehaan, its newest custodian, is desperately peddling a tale of rutting pigs, fighting mynahs, and the sorrow of the Ranikhet disease, scourge of poultry farmers. He knows he's on borrowed time—headed inexorably for that moment when someone sitting to his left shall look up at him and, almost inaudibly, mutter, 'Pass?'

If I could speak, I would urge Rehaan to take his time and savour it. But the whisky has thickened my tongue and the beedis have scorched my throat; I fear the joint might kill me. Lean back, Rehaan, and tell us the longest, juiciest story you know. Let it start from when you were two years old, scrabbling around in a sunny yard in a village in Uttar Pradesh, and stretch right up to today, twenty years later: when you have lost your virginity, started smoking, stopped speaking to your mother, fallen out with your brother, and fallen in with this lot outside this shuttered shopfront at this crossing at seven in the evening in Sadar Bazaar.

But I can't speak for fear of puking up the raw paneer and freshly boiled eggs that I ate fifteen minutes ago. Hopefully by the time Rehaan finishes his story, the pillar with the surveillance cameras will stop spinning, my seat will stop swaying, the light from the street lamps will no longer crash against my eyelashes and shatter into a thousand luminous fragments, and I may just contemplate a hit of that joint—not because I want to, no sir, but because I have to. This joint, like everything else that follows, shall be for research purposes only.

•

'I'm looking for a man named Mohammed Ashraf,' I said to a short, scruffy man who identified himself as Lalloo.

5

'I had interviewed him for a story last year. I'm from the press.'

Mohammed Ashraf is a short man, a slight man, a dark man with salt-and-pepper hair; a sharp man, a lithe man, a polite man with a clipped moustache and reddish eyes.

I first met him in December 2005 while working on a story on a proposed Delhi government bill to provide health insurance for construction workers. I had spoken with all the experts, got all my quotes, and arrived early one morning to meet some construction workers and fit their views into a story that, for all purposes, I had already written. As I recall, Ashraf had been a terrible interview subject. He had refused to answer any questions directly, choosing instead to offer up quotes like 'If you had studied psychology, you would know that if you sleep without washing your feet, you get nightmares.' After this cryptic insight he had clammed up and refused to offer his opinion on the Building and Other Construction Workers Act of 1996 and its proposed successor.

Six months later I was back in Sadar Bazaar, this time on a fellowship, searching for that very same Ashraf with the bombastic quotes. It would be a struggle to convince him to actually answer my questions, but I had time and Ashraf, as my editors and I had noted, made for excellent copy.

'Ashraf? ASHRAF!' Lalloo shouted as we picked our way through the maze of alleys behind Bara Tooti Chowk, Sadar Bazaar. 'Look what a nice angrezi murgi we've found you!'

'An AC-type murgi,' added Rehaan, a muscular young boy of about eighteen, who sidled up to the two of us, and had crushed, filled, and smoked a joint by the time we found Ashraf nursing a hangover in a shady corner of Barna Galli.

'You've come back,' said Ashraf, pulling on his beedi. 'Are you working on another story?'

'No, no,' I replied. 'This time it's a research project. I want to understand the mazdoor ki zindagi—the life of the labourer. I want to interview you some more.'

'What happened to the last one? Did you bring a cutting of your article?'

'No.'

'Well, bring it next time. Do you want some tea?'

Peering closely at the magazine I brought on my next visit, Ashraf tried not to sound disappointed. 'But this doesn't have my photo! This after you made me pose with a brush in one hand.'

'But I quoted you,' I pointed out. 'Thrice.'

'I can see that. But no photo.'

And that's how I fell in with Ashraf, Lalloo, and Rehaan. They made for an odd crew: Ashraf, the quick-witted dreamer of schemes, Lalloo, who walked with a limp and served as a foil for Ashraf's ideas, and Rehaan, the quiet boy with a smouldering joint who didn't say very much but listened to everything. It's hard to tell if they even got along, but then getting along is largely besides the point in Bara Tooti where the jokes are dark and largely unintelligible to outsiders, and conversations tangential and prone to the most unlikely non sequiturs.

'I knew this man,' Rehaan once said, apropos of nothing, 'who used to inject his testicles to get high. What do you think of that, Aman bhai?'

Nothing, Rehaan. To be honest, nothing at all.

•

'Aman bhai?' Despite his joke all those months ago about me roaming around Bara Tooti Chowk like a headless chicken, I have forgiven Rehaan. He is a polite boy. Like now, for instance, he jogs me out of my reverie and hands me the joint.

'Ah, the joint,' I mutter incoherently. I really should not take a hit of this. But after months of listening to the three complain about the perils of construction work, the horrors wreaked by the police and the sorrow of exile, this is the first time I have been invited along to do something fun. My recorder appears to have died of its own accord. Perhaps if I continue to take notes, at least some good will come of this evening.

It's getting late. On the streets beyond our sheltered niche, shops down their shutters, workers down their tools, and the world slowly heals itself in preparation for a long, bruising tomorrow. Rickshaw pullers and cigarette sellers, salesmen and repairmen, painters and plumbers, mazdoors and mistrys count out the day's wages and make their way to the liquor stores on the cornerstones of every crossing in this heaving market.

Shielded from the din of the streets, Lalloo snores gently to himself, Rehaan curls up like a baby. The joint lingers like an unanswered question. Ashraf and I sit stoned on our respective stairs, staring at each other through glazed eyes. 'It's still burning, Aman bhai. Pass?'

2

A century ago, there were no directions to Sadar Bazaar—the market was where most journeys began. One of Delhi's oldest bazars, Sadar began as a grain market on the banks of a stream that ran all the way from Haryana, right through Azad Market Chowk, past the crossing where Novelty Cinema still stands, and up towards Red Fort before joining the Yamuna river. The waterway has long been paved over; but traders talk of the urli and palli sides of Azad Market as if the bazaar were still riven by a stream rather than a noisy, throbbing strip of traffic.

Unlike the more scenic parts of the city, Sadar Bazaar shows up on tourist maps of Delhi as the large empty space between the backpacker haven of Paharganj and picturesque Chandni Chowk. Her gruff shopkeepers are wholesalers of goods shorn of glamour: plastics, metal products, raw cotton, grains. Till recently, the bazaar functioned like a small city: goods produced at one end of Sadar were stocked in shops sold at the other. After a 2004 Supreme Court order banned factory work within city limits, the factories have fallen silent, but you can still buy fizzy drinks in Choona Mandi that have been bottled in the nether regions of Paharganj.

Ashraf lives in Bara Tooti Chowk, the crossing of twelve taps, one of Sadar's road intersections. By dint of being older than most of Delhi, every lane, alleyway, and dead end in Sadar has its own claim to posterity that is kept alive by its shopkeepers, tea sellers, manual labourers, and policemen. Bara Tooti is no different.

'Mahatma Gandhi used to come here all the time,' said an old shopkeeper I once interviewed. 'He came to supervise the burning of foreign goods during the azadi andolan.'

'Did you ever see him?'

'No, no, I was just a boy then. But I did see Indira Gandhi give a speech here. She was a minister in Lal Bahadur Shastri's government. You can still see the tree she stood under. It's either the one under the shop just opposite this one, or the tree that was cut down last year.'

'The Sadar Thana down the road was the first police station in Delhi,' said a policeman standing under what could be Indira's tree. 'The angrez used it to lock up all the freedom fighters.'

'Did they ever get Gandhi?'

'Not that I would know.'

Today Bara Tooti bears few traces of Gandhi, Indira, or the imprisoned freedom fighters. And despite its name, there isn't a faucet in sight, let alone any drinking water. 'I think the taps were installed by the Mughals,' said the proprietor of Garg Sweets, a prominent confectioner at the chowk. 'I think it was the British,' said his son sitting next to him. Given that there is no trace of them, the running joke is that they must have been installed by the Municipal Corporation of Delhi.

The chowk is now one of Delhi's largest 'labour mandis', literally a labour market, on the streets of which daily wagers like Ashraf live, work, drink, and dream. To get there, I would usually ride up early mornings on my motorcycle from Connaught Place, straight past New Delhi Railway Station, under the Daryaganj flyover, along Qutb Road, before turning left through the wholesale cotton market at Rui Mandi.

On other days, I would approach the chowk from Sadar Thana Road, and stop just short of the actual intersection itself. On the left was a small structure composed of bathroom tiles that I once mistook for a public urinal—only to realize that it was, in fact, a roadside shrine. On good days, Ashraf would be sitting by the shrine with a beedi and a cup of tea, chatting up construction contractors and hustling for work. On bad days, he'd be nursing his hangover at Kaka's tea shop in an alley behind the main intersection.

Kaka's tea shop wasn't much of a shop as it was the fossilized remains of a creature formed by the inbreeding of generations of pots, pans, stoves, and cement. The shop began as a large concrete shelf—about six feet high, ten feet across, and three feet deep—fused onto the rear wall of the Aggarwal Samiti Mandir premises, but soon grew to take up most of the alleyway called Barna Galli. The temple management had leased out half the shelf to a silent machinist, who spent his day crouched on his narrow ledge with an array of lathes, wires, capacitors, and resistors for company.

On the other half lay a disused kerosene stove, a large rectangular coffee machine, a telephone, and jars of tea, coffee, sugar, cardamom, and flaky, biscuit-like 'fen'. On a large table placed adjacent to the shelf, a kettle hissed on a gas burner placed amidst glasses, teaspoons, sieves, and packets of milk. On the floor, a few feet from the table, a young boy stirred a shallow vat of milk propped up over a gas burner by a set of bricks. A second boy scurried around taking orders from workers seated all along the alley.

Sanjay 'Kaka' Kumar was a flabby forty-year-old with a salt-and-pepper beard. He sat comfortably on a plastic chair placed equidistant from all three stoves, directing his assistants with a series of precise hand gestures and the occasional curse. His tea shop was currently the subject of a legal battle between the jeweller who had built the shelf and the temple management which owned the wall on which the shelf was built. The jeweller had sublet the space out to Kaka who dutifully deposited his rent of two hundred rupees every month in court.

Bara Tooti began its day at Kaka's tea shop. The milk would arrive by five in the morning and the first batch of 'morning special' tea would be ready by a quarter past five. Ashraf and Lalloo would show up soon after and sit on a low ledge, waiting for the early morning cramps that milky tea and a beedi invariably produce.

'It's almost eight and they are still sitting here,' Kaka would exclaim irrespective of when I arrived. 'Outside at the chowk, work has come and gone, but these two are still waking up. Drink your chai, smoke your beedi, pay your two rupees for a shit, and go for work.'

'What's so special about the "morning special"?' I once asked Kaka.

'It helps build pressure,' Kaka replied. 'You understand pressure? Because a man doesn't truly wake up till he shits.'

•

If you want a job in Bara Tooti, wake up early, order a cup of chai, and wait by the main road—work will come to you. Shopkeepers looking to extend their storage space by knocking down a wall between two adjacent rooms; house owners looking to turn a balcony into an extra bedroom; contractors searching for extra labour; families looking for someone to whitewash their staircase the day before their daughter's wedding—they all come down to Bara Tooti in search of mistrys and beldaars, karigars and mazdoors.

At Bara Tooti, work is divided into 'lines' based on their perceived emphasis on skill versus strength. Tasks that require specific skills—like plumbing, carpentry, cooking, or painting—are called 'karigari' lines; these are professions where the worker must first apprentice under a master craftsman or ustad before becoming a full-fledged master himself.

A mazdoor is a general term used to describe any labourer, but mazdoori describes a much broader collection of professions. In mazdoori lines like rickshaw pullers, porters (palledars), or even helpers (who consider themselves partly of the 'helpery' line) at a roadside stall, the worker is expected to simply follow orders as efficiently and honestly as possible.

Construction offers a space for all three classes: karigar mistrys, helper beldaars, and ordinary mazdoors. A mistry, in any industry, is essentially an 'expert'; in the construction industry, his primary job is to supervise the mixing of cement, sand, and water to make concrete. It sounds like a simple job, but the recipe has to vary according to the weather, cost, and type of construction. The beldaar is the mistry's understudy. After the mistry has measured out the proportions of the masala, it is the beldaar who actually mixes the masala to make a smooth paste that is used to glue brick to brick, smoothen out floors, and strengthen the pillars that hold up the roof.

Lowest in the chain, mazdoors are responsible for carrying building materials like sand, water, or rubble, breaking down existing structures, digging trenches, or helping build the scaffolding. While a mistry makes about two hundred and fifty rupees a day, a mazdoor makes between a hundred and a hundred and fifty. However, these wages are purely indicative; at one point, when work was particularly slow, mistrys were making about one hundred and seventy-five rupees a day, while mazdoors were earning only eighty.

The raj mistry sits at the top of the hierarchy. A grizzled veteran of many years, he functions as the architect, chief engineer, and head foreman rolled into one. The raj mistry usually picks up the contract, or theka, from a house owner or shopkeeper interested in modifying a building and then recruits a team of his own comprising lesser mistrys, beldaars, and ordinary mazdoors. As the theka holder, the raj mistry keeps what's left after everyone in the workforce has been paid.

Of course, none of these categories are immutable; in times of crisis, mistrys swallow their pride and work in the trenches along with the mazdoors. When work is plentiful and mistrys are in short supply, ustads working on more than one construction site often pass on trade secrets to their understudies so that work progresses smoothly.

Mohammed Ashraf is a safediwallah. Sometimes he is a mazdoor at a construction site hauling sacks of cement up endless flights of stairs; sometimes he is a beldaar mixing the cement that mazdoors bring to him; but he sees himself primarily as a safedi karigar, a master house painter. He is not a tall man, and so, in a sense, not particularly suited to his line of work. Ideally, safediwallahs are expected to be tall and long-limbed, with slender bodies that drape themselves around ladders, and elongated arms that cover walls, shutters, and shopfronts with easy, elegant strokes.

Mohammed Ashraf is short and stubby, with a narrow but muscular chest and small, broad hands balanced on strong, flexible wrists. He is built just like a mazdoor— short, stable, and perfectly suited for lifting and carrying. But Ashraf does not grudge the throw of the dice that has made him a safediwallah with a mazdoor's body. A small man's body can do things that a slender chamak-challo cannot even contemplate.

A small man carries the ground close to him wherever he goes, even as he hangs along the side of a building three storeys high. It is the memory of the ground that allows him to crawl into crevices, perch on narrow ledges, and balance on wobbly parapets. A short man knows the limits of his body, the extent of his reach, the exact position of his centre of balance. Unlike the tall man, he holds no illusions regarding his abilities or his dimensions; he will never overreach, overextend, or overbalance.

•

In the early days, I worried that my interviews were keeping Ashraf and Lalloo from finding work, only to be assured by Ashraf that if they were wasting time talking to me, they probably weren't looking for work that day.

'Only the barsati mendaks work every day, Aman bhai,' said Ashraf. 'Not lafunters like us. We work when we feel like it.'

The barsati mendaks, the rain frogs of Bara Tooti, are the seasonal workers from villages in Delhi's neighbouring states of Uttar Pradesh, Haryana and Rajasthan. Most of them have land back home, a few acres that their fathers own, which will soon be divided among brothers.

They first come in January after the winter crop has been harvested and the fields lie fallow, and return home in time for the sowing season in July. Once sowing is complete, they return to Bara Tooti for another few months of work before heading back to the village around Diwali.

The barsati mendaks work frantically and live frugally to save as much money as they can. In the weeks leading up to Diwali they stop drinking or smoking, and save every last rupee so as to have something to show for the long absence from home. On the day before they leave, the mendaks hurriedly pay off their debts and pile into interstate buses headed homewards, leaving behind a corps of hardened Bara Tooti denizens.

Old-timers like Lalloo and Ashraf, with nowhere to go to and no one to send money to, sit by the roadside shrine I once almost pissed on, puffing on their beedis, rolling joints, and sipping whisky and water out of disposable Pepsi glasses. As Lalloo put it, 'We are old frogs now, Aman bhai, with nowhere to hop to...'

Ashraf and Lalloo met in Paharganj at a labour chowk called Choona Mandi, when Ashraf had just started work as a safediwallah. Lalloo had once worked as a mazdoor but a road accident had left him with a steel rod in his shin, rendering him incapable of heavy work. Lalloo bought a small handcart with the compensation he received and sold hot parathas to the mazdoors at the chowk.

One morning, Ashraf awoke to find Lalloo passed out beside him. 'He was completely drunk, Aman bhai. Fast asleep with his ass in the air.' The handcart was gone—lost in a game of cards to some man whose face and name were beyond Lalloo's recollection. Lalloo had sold off the remaining utensils in exchange for several bottles of alcohol and fallen into a deep sleep for nearly a day and a half. When he finally awoke, he had shed his earlier skin as a parathawallah and become a mazdoor, a metamorphosis that left him rather disturbed. Drinking with Lalloo was always unnerving; when drunk he was prone to fits of hysterical laughter that gave way to tears that rolled down his wrinkled face and vanished into his stubble.

As Ashraf would often say, with a wink of the eye and tilt of the head, 'Lalloo is a bit crack.'

•

Ashraf and Lalloo could be described as 'work oriented' rather than 'work seeking'. They usually worked for a week at a time, followed by a week of leisure financed by their earnings. Some weeks, Ashraf would make up to a thousand rupees, but he had to be careful when his money ran out.

'The worst was this one morning when I woke up—still completely drunk—and I didn't have two rupees to take a shit,' Ashraf once said when we were sitting with Rehaan and Lalloo at Kaka's. 'All my money was gone. Everything. And I didn't know where Lalloo was. I had to ask Kaka for the money—oh, the humiliation.

'"Kaka, can I have two rupees?" I ask.

'"Why two rupees, Ashraf bhai? You can have this tea for free."

'"No, tea will make it worse, I need two rupees."

'"But what can you get for two rupees these days?"

'Oh god, it was terrible.' Ashraf shuddered at the thought. 'I think I should just keep two rupees in my special pocket.'

All the clothes in Bara Tooti had special pockets for money and important papers: a breast pocket sewn on the inside of the shirt, rather than the outside; a pouch stitched into the waistband of a pair of faded trousers; an extra pocket-inside-a-pocket. Every mazdoor a walking album panelled with money, papers, phone numbers, and creased photocopies of ration cards.

Rehaan, for instance, always carried two tattered photocopies of his ration card (registered back home in Sitapur, Uttar Pradesh), a copy of his class five mark sheet that looked like it had survived a flood, a small black telephone diary, and his entire medical history in the form of a prescription for a painkiller—all secreted in various pockets on his person. In a plastic bag that never left his side, he carried a blurry X-ray of a large translucent bone gleaming against a greenish black background.

'Inside pocket, outside pocket, it doesn't make a difference if you are dead drunk on a pavement in Old Delhi,' Lalloo once said sullenly. 'You can save a thousand rupees only to have it stolen in one night. Perfectly decent young boys, who neither smoke nor drink, have awoken to find their slippers stolen in the night. Who knows where money goes in the night? In the morning there is always mazdoori.'

In the morning there will be shops to be painted, walls to be built, loads to be lifted, and trenches to be dug. There is always work on offer, but Ashraf and Lalloo have been around long enough to keep a lookout for the right job.

'The ideal job,' Ashraf once said, as if elucidating a complex mathematical function, 'has the perfect balance of kamai and azadi.' Through the course of his life, a working man must experiment with as many combinations as he can before discovering the point where these counteracting forces offset each other to arrive at a solitary moment of serenity—a point when he is both free and fortunate. At that point, a man may be excused for rocking back and forth gently, tempting fate on both sides—reaching out for that tipping point, but sliding back before his fingers touch either side. Alas, it is bliss that few, like Ashraf, attain.

'Kamai is what makes work work. Without kamai, it is not work, it is a hobby. Some call it charity; others may call it exercise—but it certainly isn't a job. A job is something a man is paid to do—and his pay is his kamai. Many of us...' Ashraf paused to stand up and take in the tea-sipping mazdoors, the gossiping mistrys, and the lazing beldaars in a smooth arc of his arm, 'many of us choose jobs only on the basis of their kamai. Six thousand rupees a month! A man could get rich with that kind of money! But they forget a crucial thing. What is that crucial thing?

'Azadi, Aman bhai, Azadi,' he continued without waiting for an answer. 'Azadi is the freedom to tell the maalik to fuck off when you want to. The maalik owns our work. He does not own us. Every morning a hundred contractors come to Bara Tooti offering permanent jobs for six thousand rupees a month. But those haramis wouldn't pay their mother six thousand rupees if she worked for them. On the first day, the contractor will give you two hundred rupees and say, "Let no one say that contractor Choduram Aggarwal doesn't pay his workers." On the second day he will do the same. But on the third day, he will give you only hundred rupees, and promise to pay you the rest later. By the end of the second week, he will pay you only a third of what he owes you. And by the end of the month, you will realize that contractor Choduram Aggarwal really does not pay his workers. But by now it is too late. You can't leave. He owes you three thousand rupees already. You are now... What are you now, Aman bhai?'

'I have no idea, Ashraf bhai.' It was clear that these questions were purely rhetorical.

'A gulam! A slave. A khacchar, a mule with neither kamai nor azadi. Which is why the best way to earn is on dehadi. If Choduram pays you on the first day, you work for him on the second. He pays on the second, work for the third. He stops paying, you stop working. After all, even if you are an LLPP, you still have your self-respect.'

'An LLPP?'

Ashraf couldn't help grinning to himself. This was classic Ashraf. There was a punchline somewhere, but he wasn't going to give it away cheap. He paused for a theatrical pull on his beedi and intoned with mock gravitas, 'In the super-specialized world of today everyone needs a degree. Some are BAs, some are MAs, some are CAs, and the truly unfortunate are PAs. The really well read are PhDs, but here on the chowk, ninety per cent of the mazdoors are LLPPs—the universal degree that we are all born with.'

'An LLPP?'

'Yes, an LLPP—Likh Lowda Padh Patthar. And when

they ask you what you are, answer loudly and proudly. Chances are they will never know what it means.'

What it means, literally, is Write Penis Read Stone—Ashrafspeak for someone who is completely illiterate. Ashraf is proud of his literacy; he can even read little bits of English. He carried a pocket-sized Hindi to English dictionary in his sling bag for years; the idea was to learn one English word a day but he never got around to doing it. Then he lost his bag.

Ashraf understands the need to appear educated. Many years ago, Ashraf had a friend who, when asked what his qualifications were, answered, 'Double BA.'

'The other party was so impressed that they gave us the contract right away.'

'So what were his degrees in, Ashraf bhai?'

'Oh, in nothing and nothing. In Bengali, we say "biye" for marriage. Raja was twice married, hence "double biye". Smart, no?'

'Brilliant.'

'In our line, we have to be brilliant,' Ashraf continued with some earnestness. 'To become a businessman you should be ready for anything, you should have answers for everything.'

To become a businessman is Ashraf's fondest dream because he believes it will free him from the clutches of a maalik forever. Even a mazdoor must answer to the man who hires him for the day; but to be a businessman, Ashraf believes, is to never have to be answerable to anyone.

Before becoming a safediwallah at Bara Tooti, Ashraf was many things in many places: he sold lemons, eggs, chickens, vests, suit lengths, and lottery tickets. He worked as a butcher, a tailor, an electrician's apprentice. He studied biology, he learnt how to repair television sets. He lived in Delhi, Bombay, Calcutta, Hyderabad, Ahmedabad, Patna, and somewhere in Punjab. But his earliest memories are of an airy house in Patna's Patliputra Colony.

3

He found it while clearing out the drawers of the old writing desk in the drawing room, next to the sofa with the shotgun. Slim, rectangular, with a grainy, textured cover, it was wrapped in clear plastic and secured with rubber bands—the thin black sort that hold the morning newspapers together in bulky rolls. A strangely familiar face stared out of the photograph on the first page.

'Who is this, Doctor saab?' Mohammed Ashraf, aged ten years, held up a fragile passport.

'That's me with a full head of hair.'

'What is this for?'

'It's for going to America.'

In 1947, Syed Mustapha Hussain went to America to complete his PhD at the University of Michigan. 'That too on full scholarship. I told Nehru, "This country needs two things: farmers and scientists."'

'You knew Pandit Nehru?'

'Of course. Back then, everyone knew everyone.'

Upon his return in the 1950s, Dr Hussain settled in Patna and rose to considerable prominence in the Department of Animal Husbandry. Depending on which interview tape I consult, Ashraf came to Dr Hussain's house when he was five/eight/ten with his mother Sakina and his younger brother Aslam from their village in the Guraru taluk of Bihar's Gaya district. His father died when Ashraf was just one/two/three; Ashraf has few memories of his father except that he 'did something with the railways' and was rarely home.

In Patna, Sakina found work with Dr Hussain. Right from the beginning, Ashraf loved Dr Hussain. He still remembers his address, 207 Patliputra Colony.

Dr Hussain taught Ashraf how to clean a shotgun and told him stories about going on shikar and hunting leopards. Dr Hussain took Ashraf to Hyderabad when he went to visit his daughter. During the trip, when Ashraf suddenly developed a sharp pain in his molars, Dr Hussain took him to the best dentist in Hyderabad, who pulled out Ashraf's tooth for free just because he respected Dr Hussain. Dr Hussain insisted Ashraf go to school and occasionally helped him with his homework. Dr Hussain told Ashraf that if he studied hard and did well enough, maybe he could go America too and become a doctor like Dr Hussain.

Till he was sixteen, Ashraf's life kept pace with Dr Hussain's dreams; he finished high school and enrolled in a biology programme at Patna's Magadh University. He sat in class with the 'mummy–daddy' type children whose mummies would pack their lunch and daddies would pick them up after class. No one made lunch for Ashraf and in the evenings he hurried home to help out; but he still studied twice as hard as everyone else.

Then, one evening in February, a few months before his exams, he was startled by the sound of a determined thumping on the front door.

•

Rinse rat in water and place on dissection tray on dorsal side.

Pin limbs to dissection tray.

Make first incision along the vertical axis, bisecting the rat from abdomen to chin.

Take care to cut only skin, avoiding damage to major veins and arteries.

'Just the skin, just the skin,' muttered Ashraf as he struggled to memorize the instructions. Cut a vein by accident and the tray becomes a mess of bright red roohafza-coloured water.

Lift the rat's skin with the forceps and pin to dissection tray.

What was that noise?

Studying in his room on the terrace, Ashraf was disturbed by a commotion on the first floor. Someone was banging on the front door. Someone was kicking the door hard enough to shake dust from its frame.

Locate the thymus gland which is placed over the anterior portion of the heart. Carefully move it out of the way.

He looked over the side of the terrace, still murmuring the dissection procedure under his breath.

Using forceps, carefully cut muscle and fatty tissue away from major arteries.

It was Taneja, the tenant from the ground floor—Taneja and a gang of men. They were hammering away at the ageing door; it would not hold for much longer. Dr Hussain was shouting. He was shouting, 'Idiot, nonsense fellow,' as loudly as he could. The men were laughing loudly. This was a strictly 'Bhenchod, chootiya' group.

The men had guns.

Fuck, Fuck, Fuck.

The men had guns!

Dr Hussain had a gun.

Dr Hussain had a shotgun on the sofa near the writing desk.

The stairs from the terrace to the back door of the kitchen were steep. Check the table near the balcony. The pellets were in the small drawer under the radio set.

They had not noticed, they could not notice. Dr Hussain was still shouting in the hall. Stand in the balcony, must stand in the balcony. Remember what Dr Hussain had said about the shikar, the time he almost shot a leopard. Stand firm, keep your feet planted, take a deep breath. Don't tremble. Don't tremble. Stop trembling! Aim carefully. Squeeze the trigger gently, no jerky movements, just like squeezing a lemon, only a little firmer. Ready, Aim, Fire!

Not Ready!

Can't Aim!

Aim at Anything!

Aim! Shoot! Fire!

Shoot! Aim!

Shoot!

Just Shoot!

He pulled the trigger. The butt of the ancient shotgun recoiled violently, slipping off Ashraf's shoulder and crashing against his ribs with a dull thud. Dazed and deafened, Ashraf stared down at the garden: the pellets had ripped a jagged hole in the canopy of the banyan tree. Taneja and his cohorts stood motionless as tiny shredded leaves fluttered down around them like wedding confetti.

Taneja was the first to look up. Ashraf was shouting incoherently, tears streaming down his face. His shaking hands cradled Dr Hussain's favourite shotgun, its sights pointed squarely at Taneja. The double-barrelled shotgun quivered, as if anticipating another explosion. Taneja turned around and walked back into the house; the hoodlums slipped into their vehicles and zoomed off in a cloud of dust. Ashraf returned the gun to its place next to the side table and went back to his study.

If all steps are carried out correctly, the student should be able to see the rat's beating heart.

•

'Subhash Chandra Taneja was tall and fair. He was a Punjabi just like you,' says Ashraf, as if I am somehow responsible for the conduct of this man. 'People used to say he looked a bit like Feroz Khan.

'But people also told us he was an honest man who would be a good tenant. People will say anything that comes into their heads.

'People are chootiyas,' he concludes.

Of course, Ashraf knew all along that Taneja was not to be trusted. Because Ashraf knows everything. 'I told Dr Hussain when they made out the lease: never trust Punjabis. But no one listens to me.' Except for me it seems. I have been listening to Ashraf for two hours this morning, and haven't got a word in edgeways.

'Taneja was a smuggler. He ran an auto parts business out of a showroom on Exhibition Street, but he simply bought fake Chinese parts from the Nepal border and sold them at the same prices as the real thing. Once he got into Dr Hussain's house he was never going to go away.

'If I thought like you presswallahs think, I would probably say Taneja was the reason I ended up at Bara Tooti. He would probably find it really funny that after all these years, you and I, sitting here in Delhi, are talking about him.

'Yes, he would. He was that kind of chootiya. Before I met Taneja—I was a good boy, studying first year biology at Magadh University, hoping to become some sort of officer. But Taneja didn't send me here. Maybe I was coming all along; I just needed something to show me the way.'

Ashraf first mentioned Taneja many months after I began plotting his route from Patna to Delhi.

'So why did you leave Patna?' I would ask with admirable persistence.

'Kuch ho gaya tha, something happened,' he would say dismissively before suddenly turning my attention to something else. 'Look at that man negotiating with a contractor—that contractor is a very big man; some say he almost became a minister in Madanlal Khurana's sarkar.

'See that tree near the corner? That one with the poster? That's Indira's tree. I'm sure of it.'

'Why did you leave Patna, Ashraf bhai?'

'Something happened. See that man using that fine chisel—we call that an asula...'

And so it would continue: me pointing my recorder at Ashraf and asking questions, Ashraf deflecting them by distracting me with chowk trivia: 'You know why rickshaw pullers are usually Biharis? Because no one else can afford to be one; Biharis can live more cheaply than anyone else. I'm a Bihari, I know these things.'

Occasionally, Ashraf would reward my persistence with a straight answer.

'Taneja! Taneja, Taneja, Taneja... Taneja wanted Dr Hussain's house. You may not know this, but in many towns there are people—harami types—who keep an eye out for houses like Dr Hussain's: a house where a retired person's middle-aged son has unexpectedly died; someone's children have left for another city; a wife of fifty years has a heart attack. So the old man will say, "What will I do alone in this big house?" and that's when they strike.'

Taneja appeared one morning, soon after Dr Hussain's only daughter and her husband had left for Hyderabad. By the afternoon he had convinced Dr Hussain to take him in as a tenant. In the evening, Ashraf was sent along to buy stamp paper to formalize the lease.

'Bas, in two months Taneja refused to pay rent, and in the third month he tried to throw Dr Hussain out of his own house. That's when the aasmani firing took place, when I fired the gun in the air.'

In the fourth month Dr Hussain took Taneja to court.

In the seventh month a car suddenly veered off the road and knocked Dr Hussain down when the old man was out on his evening walk. He was rushed to the Holy Family Hospital, but the doctors were pessimistic about his chances.

'Even there he was surrounded by Punjabis—one Dr Bhatia. Taneja was also a Punjabi. All these Punjabis in Bihar—they were all united. One Punjabi will never cross another Punjabi. You should know... The moment I saw him, I knew he would try something—and he did. He stopped Dr Hussain's heart medication.

'How can you do that? You tell me, Aman bhai, would you stop his heart medication?'

'No, Ashraf bhai. No, I wouldn't. Also, I'm only half Punjabi. My grandfather insists he is actually Pathan.'

'Hmm. You certainly look somewhat Pathan.' But he isn't going to forgive me just yet. 'Sethi! What kind of name is Sethi?'

'Well, it's a Punjabi name, but my family...'

'Sethi is a Punjabi name!' he interrupts. 'Deep down you are all Punjabis.'

'An entrepreneurial race,' he adds as an afterthought, 'but very cunning. Not like us Biharis.'

On the fourth day after the attack, Ashraf received a frantic phone call urging him to come to the hospital immediately. Dr Hussain had refused to take his medicines. Ashraf arrived to find a grimly determined Dr Hussain fending off all efforts to feed him. Ashraf held Dr Hussain's hands and coaxed him into accepting a bowl of cornflakes. The old man sat up in bed for the first time since his admission and clenched Ashraf's hands tightly—as if to ward off a spasm. Ashraf stood by the bed, talking as fast as he could in his most reassuring tone.

'Cornflakes, Doctor saab—cornflakes and milk, warm milk. Cornflakes and warm milk, with sugar—just a little sugar. For energy, sugar gives us energy.'

Talking faster and faster he wiped away the milk that had dribbled out of Dr Hussain's mouth, assured him that the medicines were already working, that Dr Hussain was already looking much stronger. 'I checked; your passport is still valid. Once you get out we'll leave this place and go for a holiday to America. But for that you need to eat, Doctor saab, please eat. You need to swallow these pills, you need to drink enough water, you need to...'

Dr Hussain waved his hand as if to silence Ashraf; his grip on Ashraf's hands slowly slackened and a perfect stillness filled the room.

Dr Hussain was buried in a quiet ceremony in Patna. There was no close male relative in the family, and so the body, which had to be washed as per custom, was bathed by Ashraf. The last rites were completed in the presence of the local maulvi, the shrouded figure was lowered into the grave, and laid on its right side in the direction facing Mecca.

A few days after the funeral, a policeman accosted Ashraf on the street. 'Taneja has not forgotten the firing. Be careful, Ashraf, there have been a lot of car accidents lately.'

A month later, Mohammed Ashraf packed his clothes, his books, and his dissection kit and left Patna.

'What about college, Ashraf bhai?'

'What about college, Aman bhai? I was so stressed that I forgot to register for my second year exams. Then, the house got sold. I said to myself, "Forget college, Ashraf. We need a roof over our heads." My mother found a house in the jhuggi, I needed a job, so I dropped out.'

'You don't believe me, do you?' Ashraf looks uncomfortable. Rather than quelling my curiosity, the story of Ashraf's childhood has prompted a barrage of questions: How old were you? How did you get admission? Couldn't you re-enroll? What did your mother think?

On and on, I fired away till finally I made my first big mistake.

'Are you sure you are talking about going to college and not school, Ashraf bhai?'

'What do you think? I may be a mazdoor, but I can tell the difference between school and college. I have sliced open frogs with my own hands.'

'No, not for a minute am I suggesting... All I am saying is...' But it is too late. Ashraf is very annoyed.

For many weeks thereafter, Ashraf would intersperse his conversation with me with the occasional nugget of trivia. 'This cigarette you are smoking, the active ingredient is nicotine. Nicotine is also used as pesticide. It is very bad for your health.'

'Thank you, Ashraf.'

'It's fine. Your tea has—what was it?—coffee? No, no, caffeine. Too much caffeine is not good for your health either.'

'That's great, Ashraf bhai.'

'I just remembered a lesson from my first year biology, that's all. Funny how you remember these things all of a sudden.'

4

On a blazing afternoon in June, Ashraf and his cohorts
retired to one of the shady alleyways surrounding Bara
Tooti. It was too hot to work, too hot to drink, too hot
to sleep, and since there is little else to do at the chowk,
mazdoors sat around swapping stories in a desultory,
disinterested manner that went something like this:

'It's so hot, yaar...'

'This is nothing. Once I was travelling between Lucknow
and Kanpur in the month of May... That day it was so hot
the floor of the bus was chaka-chak with sweat...'

'Lucknow? I didn't know you were from Lucknow...'

'I'm not, I'm from Meerut...'

'It must get really hot in Meerut...'

'Not as hot as here...'

'God, it's so hot...'

Most stories are travellers' tales, beginning with a bus,

truck, or train ride and ending with, '…and then I came to Bara Tooti, and it has been the same ever since.'

Ashraf tells me one of his favourite stories—that of his first night in Delhi, when, for him, the city was still a mysterious place of freedom, camaraderie, and possibility.

'I arrived on the late night train from Surat, Gujarat, around half past nine, at Old Delhi Railway Station. I had nothing on me. Absolutely nothing. One bundle of clothes and maybe two or three beedis.

'On the train someone had said that in Delhi, the police harassed those who slept on railway platforms, so I thought I would sleep outside Jama Masjid. But the guard told me that the masjid was closed for the night. I slipped into one of the lanes near the masjid and I saw some people playing cards.

'You should always ask permission before approaching a group of card players because if any money goes missing later, they will always blame it on you. So I said, "Bhaiya, I'm new to this place. Can I sleep somewhere around here?" They looked up. One of them said, "Have you eaten?" I shook my head. He pressed a five-rupee coin into my hand and pointed me towards a stall.

'I ate, bought some beedis, unrolled my sheet, and fell asleep right there on the pavement.'

When he awoke the next morning, the city was already wide awake. Last night's card players had disappeared, as had the food stall, the beedi seller, and even the security guard. Only Jama Masjid remained where it had been last night, its onion-shaped domes reassuring in their solidity.

Ashraf spent the first week exploring the city, searching out work and places to sleep. 'And then I found Bara Tooti and it has been the same ever since,' Ashraf concludes with a wry smile.

'But if Delhi is such a boring place, why does anyone even come here?' I ask.

'It's hard to say, Aman bhai. Everyone has their own special reasons, personal reasons, family reasons, emotional reasons. You can't just go around asking people why they are here.

'There is something Delhi can give you—a sense of azadi, freedom from your past. Everyone knows Delhi. Delhi has Qutub Minar, Red Fort, Old Fort. For every person who makes a bit of money in Delhi, an entire village arrives in search of work. So if you are leaving home, you might as well come to Delhi. Where else would a runaway run away to?'

One summer afternoon, I met a painter called Idris who claimed that he came away to Delhi after he shot someone with a country-made pistol.

'Did you kill him?'

'No, that was the biggest mistake. He survived and now he wants to kill me.

'There are just two types of people here,' he said, pulling me close. 'Those who pull the trigger, and those who survive the shootout. Goli maar ke bhi log aate hain. Goli kha ke bhi log aate hain.'

I looked past him at the gaggle of mazdoors fanning themselves in the heat. If only each one of them was a gunslinging mercenary on the run, I thought wistfully.

•

J.P. Singh Pagal is a man who tells Delhi stories better than most. He is short, slender, and hyperactive, with enormous eyes that constantly goggle, as if he were seeing the world for the first time.

J.P. appeared one day at Bara Tooti, weaving through the crowd of exhausted mazdoors, pulling furiously on his chillum, exhaling plumes of bittersweet marijuana, interrupting conversations, pushing, shoving, joking, bitching, shouting, and laughing his curious ascending laugh.

Tales of unexplained disappearances, stories of amazing good fortune, whispers of a strange dark creature that prowls the eastern borders of the city—J.P. Singh knew them all and had seen them all. 'Watch out, it's the half-man-half-machine-half-monkey-fully-dangerous Monkeyman. I was there, beedu, I saw him and I screamed! Just like the lady who dropped her pallu in fright; just like the man who killed his sister and threw her body in the gutter. I saw them all, haha, HaHa, HAHA!

'And what's this? A recorder? Gathering evidence?'

'No, no, I'm just a reporter.'

'You say you are a reporter. I say you are a policeman. Haha, HaHa, HAHA!'

Nonetheless, he sat down beside me and reduced my cunning interview technique to shambles.

Aman: So Ravi bhai, would you say that building a house is more art than a craft?

Ravi: Er...

J.P. Singh: Tell us, Ravi—you son of a randi. Is it an art or a craft? What are your views on quality versus quantity? Tell us, tell us, you chootiya. Did you know they found a condom in a Pepsi bottle? A used one! Haha. I put it there. And the fire in Meerut? I was carrying the matches. The woman whose clothes fell off in the Fashion Week, the bomb that went off, the film with Dino Morea and that londiya—I always forget her name...

A: You made it?

J.P.: (in all seriousness) I made it.

My recordings from that day are littered with J.P.'s comments on me, my work, and everyone I met. He followed me around for hours as I walked the chowk asking undeniably boring questions. For instance, this clip on 'How to build a house':

A: How do you pass time while building a house?
Mazdoor: We work.
A: But you think of things while you work?
Mazdoor: Everyone does.
A: What do you think of?
Mazdoor: I think of work when I work.

J.P., in the meantime, provided background chatter, humming around my ears like an irate wasp. As I sought new insights into the condition of labour, he distracted my subjects by passing on news—'Dino Morea's new movie is called *Raaz*. It's a hit!'; handing out insults—'Arre chootiya, answer the question;' and spreading paranoia—'You see those security cameras over there? There, you chootiya, up there. It's recording your every move, it has a microphone that tapes what you say. You see that small shop behind it? That's where the riot police lie resting. A word from the control room and they will burst out with sticks and guns to hit you and shoot you and beat you into pulp.'

Elsewhere, when I asked a man about his favourite building:

J.P.: You know of the Taj Mahal?
Mazdoor: Yes.
J.P.: Did you know Shah Jahan cut off the hands of everyone who worked on it?

M: No.

J.P.: Do you know if it still happens around here?

M: No...

J.P.: Trust me, it happens.

When I finally gave up, we sat down for a smoke: me with my cigarettes—no more beedis; after a year in Bara Tooti, I realized being one of the boys is an experiment fraught with peril—and he with his chillum. Time passed. I smoked my cigarette down to the filter and lit another. I felt I should ask J.P. a few questions—he would be great for the book—but I couldn't bring myself to. But what if I never saw him again? Suddenly I was exhausted.

J.P. Singh leaned over and handed me a photograph. Shot in a studio, it captured a young, dashing J.P., astride a stationary motorcycle arranged against a painted backdrop that seemed to be whizzing past. He looked happy; a shapely feminine hand rested on his shoulder. From the angle of the handle, I deduced she must be sitting sideways 'ladies-style', also facing the camera. I 'deduced', as the photograph had been neatly torn in two, excising J.P.'s companion (and the rear wheel of the bike) from the frame. When I asked him about the photograph, he snatched it from my hand. 'The world changed, and so did we,' he sang mournfully and slipped away into the evening's gathering darkness.

J.P. was right; the world was changing, an imperceptible hysteria was pulsing through the city. For as long as I can remember, Delhi looked like a giant construction site inhabited by bulldozers, cranes, and massive columns of prefabricated concrete; but the rubble has masked the incredible changes and dislocations of factories, homes, and livelihoods that occurred as Delhi changed from a sleepy north Indian city into a glistening metropolis of a rising Asian superpower. Working class settlements like Yamuna Pushta, Nangla Machi, and Sanjay Amar Colony were flattened by government demolition squads to make way for broader roads, bigger power stations, and the Commonwealth Games.

Before he settled down on a footpath in Bara Tooti, Ashraf lived in Sanjay Amar Colony, a settlement on the western bank of the Yamuna river.

'When I arrived in Delhi, I did all kinds of work—I worked in a meat shop, I travelled to Punjab with a construction crew, I did mazdoori at Bara Tooti. I did anything I could find and slept wherever I found space.

'Then one day, I found work with a Masterji who stitched sports sets. Some company gave him pre-cut pieces of cloth which we stitched into shorts and vests.'

It was a big company that outsourced its stitching to hundreds of workers across Delhi and exported the finished products to Dubai. Every month a company representative would come to Masterji's tiny two-room house-cum-workshop, pick up the stitched garments, and drop off fresh supplies for the coming month.

'There were just two of us with our sewing machines, Masterji and I. For two, maybe three years, we lived together, ate together, and worked together. The work was easy, my clothes were always neat, clean, and well tailored. It was great.'

Then in 2004, a bulldozer drove up to Sanjay Amar Colony and razed it to the ground.

'We had heard of demolition drives across the city, but we never thought it would happen to us,' Ashraf says. In the first drive, more than 150,000 homes were demolished. Eventually, about 350,000 houses would be levelled as part of a beautification drive launched by a cabal of government agencies.

'The demolition ruined Masterji. He didn't have a title for his land and so never got any compensation. Two days after the demolition, he packed his bags and went back to Bengal. I gathered my clothes and came to Bara Tooti.'

'Was this the first time you came to Bara Tooti?'

'No, no. I had lived here intermittently for many years before I started work with Masterji. When he left, I moved here full-time.'

Ashraf says that despite its name, Sanjay Amar Colony was a largely Muslim settlement. 'That's why it was one of the first to go. That year, 2004, was an election year and the BJP was in power. They knew that the basti would vote for the Congress, so they thought, "Let's demolish the Muslim areas first."'

It didn't work, the Congress still came to power, but for Ashraf, and thousands like him, it was little consolation.

'The BJP just lost the elections. We lost our lives.'

The violent displacement of 800,000 slum dwellers received surprisingly little attention in the national press that described the process as a necessary and painful part of urban renewal. But occasionally, the working class city would force its way into the daily news in bizarre and mysterious ways. From 2000 onwards, there were a series of unlikely incidents—the appearance of fantastic creatures, the rise of serial killers like West Delhi's Hammerman, and a mysterious masked motorcyclist who dressed in black and prowled Delhi's streets by night—that could just have been made up by J.P. Singh Pagal but were reported in national dailies.

In the summer of 2001, for instance, an elusive creature was spotted in working class dwellings in Ghaziabad and

East Delhi's adjoining districts. Descriptions varied between a primitive four-foot-tall humanoid, and a futuristic, if somewhat hirsute, robot from outer space. When public hysteria reached fever pitch, the Delhi Police commissioned a study on the phenomenon, hoping that a report that categorically denied the existence of the creature would put an end to the phenomenon.

If the testimonies of fifty-five witnesses, interviewed by the Institute of Human Behaviour and Allied Sciences, are compiled, the Monkeyman was a creature between four and eight feet tall with long iron legs shod in sleek black sneakers with springs attached to the soles.

On closer examination, he was observed to have long hair, a 'terrible face', which he sometimes masked, and gleaming lasers for eyes. He struck mostly at night, though one witness claimed to have been attacked at 10:15 am; and could be identified by his distinctive call of 'ohu-ohu', 'she-she', or 'ho-ho', depending on the witness interviewed. Apart from his ability to jump great distances, the Monkeyman sometimes flew with the help of a black belt, a red-and-black-striped suit, and a light affixed to his chest. 'He was like Shaktimaan,' noted an excitable young woman, before she swooned and fainted into the arms of a troubled behavioural scientist.

I met Dr Nimesh Desai, the lead author of the study on the Monkeyman, over a cup of coffee in the genteel settings of the India International Centre on Max Mueller Marg. My purpose was to understand what such stories told us about the city we lived in. Dr Desai stroked his beard and offered me a biscuit. 'The problem with the Monkeyman issue was that, in at least one case, someone had been attacked by a real monkey.'

But it was the other cases that were more interesting. Almost everyone interviewed by Dr Desai had claimed to have tried to grab the creature. 'So the scratch marks should have been on the ventral aspect of the forearm'—for any creature caught and clawing to get away would leave long gashes on the inner part of the forearm. However, 'all scratches were along the dorsal aspect, that is, the outer part of the forearm, suggesting', Dr Desai leaned over the elegant teapot, 'that the injuries were self-inflicted!'

Dr Desai stressed that this was only a preliminary hypothesis but he surmised that most of the victims were going through considerable amounts of stress at the time. Some had known histories of substance abuse, some were worried by the threat of eviction or demolition of their houses, some had absent husbands and ill family members, and many were characterized, by researchers, as having severe sleep deprivation and 'histrionic personas' (a tendency to be excessively emotional and attention hungry).

When the news of the creature broke, it was possible that the victims had attributed to the Monkeyman injuries that they had unknowingly inflicted on themselves in their sleep.

'It could be mass hysteria caused by mass media,' he concluded.

Dr Desai's report lay on my desk for many days: a snap-shot of a city splintering under the strain of a fundamental urban reconfiguration—a city of the exhausted, distressed, and restless, struggling with the uncertainties of eviction and unemployment; a city of twenty million histrionic personas resiliently absorbing the day's glancing blows only to return home and tenderly claw themselves to sleep.

•

By ferreting out the absurd, the unlikely, and the almost true, J.P. Singh Pagal served as the medium for Delhi's dislocation and unease. His stories seemed informed by the newspapers, street gossip, and his unique perspective that was in turn framed by a deep-seated paranoia directed against the government and police. In the course of their work, the mazdoors of Bara Tooti travelled across the city, picking up snippets of information that they used to measure the 'temperature' of the city. 'Mahaul garam hai, the situation is hot,' said a mazdoor once when I asked him about the mood in a slum settlement that had just been demolished by the Delhi Municipal Corporation.

J.P. Singh tapped into this network of mazdoor information and passed on the news as he travelled from chowk to chowk in the markets of the old city. With J.P., as with any tabloid, it was enough to know that 'something had happened' in a certain part of Delhi. The specifics of the incident could always be sought from a more reliable source.

Sadly, I never met J.P. Singh again, but everyone in Bara Tooti had a J.P. Singh story. 'He's a thief!' proclaimed Rehaan with uncharacteristic vehemence. 'He's the man who steals chappals in the night.'

'Have you ever caught him, Rehaan?'

'No, obviously not. He's so good at it that no one has ever caught him.'

'So how do you know it's him?'

'I just know.'

Lalloo had an amazing story about him. 'J.P. Singh was not always like this,' he said. 'Once upon a time he was a very big man—in Bollywood. He used to roam around with all the actors and actresses and he used to drink English whisky.'

J.P. used to work in the Sadar Bazaar office of a major Bombay film producer where his primary job was to make sure the office stayed neat and clean in case someone ever visited. 'But no one visited,' according to Lalloo. 'So all he did was sit in the office and get drunk. Sometimes when he was bored of drinking alone, he would come down to Bara Tooti and drink with us. Sometimes if he got too drunk, he would pass out here on the pavement amongst us.'

Then one day, the film producer finally did visit—but J.P. wasn't there. 'He was fast sleep in the galli behind Kaka's shop—drunk out of his mind. The producer was very angry, but because J.P. was basically a good man, the producer took him along to Bombay.'

In Bombay, J.P. worked as a handyman on Bollywood sets. 'Whenever he was back in Delhi, he used to drop in. After a few drinks, he would boast about meeting this actress and putting makeup on that actress's face—Aishwarya Rai, Sushmita Sen, Karishma, everyone. But once when he was very drunk, he burst into tears and confessed.'

It was true that J.P. was working in Bollywood, but his job was to supervise the daily wage workers who built the sets, mark their attendance, and pay them their seventy-five rupees at the end of each day. 'He was working in Bollywood, but he wasn't meeting any actresses. He spent his day among chootiyas like us.' Lalloo couldn't help the broad smile that spread across his face. 'Aishwarya, Sushmita, lowda mera. J.P. was a munshi at a construction site!'

A few months later, he returned to Bara Tooti. 'By now he was beginning to look a little crazed. He had fallen out with his employer once and for all and told us he would never go back to Bombay.'

'So what did he do, Lalloo bhai?'

'I don't know. Every time he came, he seemed a little

more insane. Finally someone saw him sleeping behind a shop in Khari Baoli and we realized he was now living on the streets in Chandni Chowk.

'We still see him around occasionally. But every time he comes, something goes missing. It is difficult, no, Aman bhai? If a man loses everything in one go, what option does he have but to go mad? At least we only lose things in stages.'

No one really sees J.P. any more, but ever so often someone's slippers go missing in the night and they wake up and remember J.P. Singh Pagal, the half-mad teller of half-true tales.

•

It's 2 am and my phone's ringing. It happens every now and then; it's usually Ashraf, and he's usually drunk. There is an all-night phone booth near Old Delhi Railway Station. I imagine Ashraf slurring unconcernedly as a crowd of irate railway passengers wait for him to finish.

'Aman sirji, I hope it's not too late to call, but Ashraf wants to say "hello".'

'Hello, Ashraf.'

'Hello, Aman bhai. Were you sleeping?'

'Yes.'

'Ah. I just called to say that yesterday a girl came to the chowk and asked me how many mazdoors are there in this chowk. So I said, "Fifty." So she said, "Make them stand in line." So I made them stand in line. Then she gave us all ten rupees and went away. Hello? Are you there?'

'Uh-huh.'

'It's late, isn't it?'

'Yes, Ashraf bhai.'

'I just called because I thought this might interest you—for your research, you know. Anyway, we were all just drinking and thinking of you. I thought, why not call you?'

'Why not indeed.'

'Good night, Aman bhai.'

'Good night, Ashraf.'

two
AKELAPAN,
or Solitude

1

In the spring of 1992, Munna borrowed a bicycle from his mother's sister's brother-in-law, who owned a cycle shop in Chandni Chowk. It was the day before Holi. Summer was still some weeks off, but the sun was hot enough to give dull headaches to those foolish enough to step out of the shade for too long.

Pedalling along with long, easy strokes, he made good time as he headed out beyond Old Delhi Railway Station down towards the river to meet a friend who lived trans-Yamuna. Onward he went down the outer Ring Road, past the many Hanuman mandirs, under the imposing arches of Red Fort. Children were already out in the streets, jump-starting celebrations that would continue till noon the next day. At the gurdwara on the way, he contemplated stopping for langar—it was now past twelve and devotees would soon be handing out lunch to the pious and the poor—but decided to press on.

He finally stopped at Shastri Park, just short of the turn towards the Wazirpur Barrage, and dismounted for a quick drink of water. Excise laws prohibit the sale of alcohol before noon; but all thekas, including the one at Shastri Park, open their counters by one o'clock. The Shastri Park theka was a bit of a 'last chance' theka—beyond the Wazirpur Barrage, Delhi's distinct borders dissolved into an intermittent patchwork of East Delhi and West Uttar Pradesh, each square corresponding to different excise duties, fuel prices, and telephone exchanges. But the Shastri Park theka was unequivocally in Delhi; and as Delhi sells some of the cheapest alcohol in north India, this was an important distinction.

He lingered around the theka, eyeing the bottles that peeked out from behind the shop's iron grille front. He stared at the brown paper bags stuffed under the arms of those leaving the store. Why buy rum at fifty rupees a half in UP when he could buy it here for just thirty-five? Whisky was at seventy-five, beer at thirty-five, Jalwa country liquor at only twenty-five. How much money did he have? A brisk appraisal of the contents of his pockets suggested he had 'enough'—kaafi. Not 'just about enough', but closer to a 'more than enough'—enough with an emphasis.

Perhaps he could simply stock up and continue on his way. But it was really hot. Maybe a quick quarter, followed by an even quicker nap, and a resumption of the journey by about four when things had cooled off a bit? But if he was drinking, instead of a quarter of Jalwa, he could perhaps have a half of rum? Rum could be considered a light drink—well, not exactly light, maybe lightish—definitely lightish compared to Jalwa. And he wouldn't smoke a beedi—because it was beedis that got people high. Without a beedi the alcohol stays in the stomach; with a beedi, the heat makes it vaporize and enter the brain. Or was it the other way around—did alcohol make beedis enter the brain? But in either case, beedis were bad for the brain, and alcohol was good for the heart. 'After Holi I shall not smoke beedis,' he resolved and, fortified with piety, thrust his hand under the barricaded front onto the shop's countertop. 'A half bottle of rum.'

By the time the rum wore off, four o'clock had long passed him by. The sky looked decidedly sixish, as did the torrent of rush hour traffic on the bridge. He hurried down to the bus stop near the bridge and hopped onto the first bus he saw. Still woozy, he stuck his head out of the window, watching as the driver expertly negotiated cars, buses, tractors, and swarms of bicycles. Bicycles? Wait, he had a bicycle. In fact, he had his mother's sister's brother-in-law's bicycle. But he seemed to be travelling by bus.

Bhenchod!

Harried commuters on the Wazirpur Barrage that evening pressed down hard on their brakes as an Uttar Pradesh Roadways bus screeched to a halt in the middle of the road. Suddenly, the door swung open and he jumped out into the oncoming traffic. A second later, the driver poked his head out, delivered a stream of abuse, and the bus lurched on towards Ghaziabad. Embarrassed but unhurt, he rose to his feet, smiled sheepishly at the piled-up traffic, and made his way back to Shastri Park.

'I left a bicycle here a few hours ago.'

The man behind the counter peered out from his self-imposed internment. The thick steel grille that protected him from his customers obstructed his view of anything that did not occur directly in front of him. Out here on the frontier, it was best not to see anything at all. People did the stupidest things under the influence of alcohol, and if he saw everything that happened on the perimeters of his theka he would have to give up his business and become a full-time witness. But the grille had fixed all that; he had survived three years without seeing a single thing. So when Munna enquired about the whereabouts of his bicycle, the man behind the counter at first pretended not to see him at all. But after a while it became impossible to ignore the persistent banging on the steel grille.

'I left a bicycle here a few hours ago.'

'I left one too. Can you see it?' said the man behind the counter.

'No.'

'They must have left together. Goodnight.'

Misplacing a bicycle is a pretty serious oversight—especially if it belongs to one's mother's sister's brother-in-law. He would have thought that the owner of a cycle shop would be reasonably relaxed when it came to lending out bicycles—particularly to family members—but no, not this man. Short of making Munna sign an affidavit rendering him a gulaam for the rest of his life, he had mobilized the pride of entire branches of their shared family tree, promising to humiliate him in front of the whole clan if he as much as punctured a tyre. He probably cursed me from the start, Munna thought; serves the bastard right. Thus filled with righteous indignation, he walked back to the Interstate Bus Terminal at Kashmere Gate and caught the night bus to Panipat.

At Panipat he changed buses for Amroha. At Amroha he stayed at his sister's house and plied a rickshaw. When his sister tired of his company, he moved to Moradabad where he worked as a painter for a few years before saving enough to get married. His family was overjoyed by the prospect of him finally settling down. But a year later, for no obvious reason, he jumped onto a bus and arrived at the Inter State Bus Terminal near Kashmere Gate. As he walked down from Kashmere Gate to Bara Tooti, Munna realized it had been ten years since that day before Holi. By now his uncle would surely have forgotten about the bicycle.

•

Munna has been summoned by Ashraf to Kaka's tea shop to explain to me how and why he came to Bara Tooti. According to Ashraf, Munna's story illustrates that the life of the mazdoor is equal parts azadi and akepalan, or solitude. 'Today I can be in Delhi,' says Ashraf. 'Tomorrow I could well be in a train halfway across the country; the day after, I can return. This is a freedom that comes only from solitude. Isn't that so, Munna?'

'Yes, Ashraf bhai.' Munna is a slender, reedy mistry with salt-and-pepper hair, his lungs hollowed out by smoking, his voice a throaty whisper. His matchstick arms are encased in plaster casts—a consequence of a drunken argument with a policeman who knocked him out without much ado.

When Munna came to, he was in the public ward of the Bara Hindu Rao Hospital in Malkaganj with both his hands in slings. 'So I slipped out of the ward and hurried back here.'

'Didn't you meet a doctor, ask a nurse? Find out what happened?'

'I couldn't find anyone. Besides, I didn't have any money for the plaster cast. So I ran away without paying.'

'It's a government hospital, Munna. They weren't going to charge you a per square foot rate for the plaster of Paris in your cast.'

'Oh, and how was I supposed to know that?'

I am flummoxed by the manner in which Ashraf and his friends make decisions.

'Why did you come back, Munna?'

'I felt like it, Aman bhai. I missed Delhi.'

'But what about your wife?'

'I suppose I miss her too, but I keep going back.'

'When did you last go?'

'Three years ago.'

Ashraf is frowning. I think I've asked too many questions. It's bad form to keep asking people about pasts that they are reluctant to confront. At Bara Tooti people come and go all the time. A man could get up from a drinking session, walk down the road for a piss, keep walking till he reached the railway station, hop onto a train, and return after a year without anyone really missing him.

I suspect Ashraf sees himself as that man, the sort who jumps onto a train on a whim and is carried away to a faraway place. Ashraf loves the railways; he can talk about them forever. Stations, train numbers, timings, junctions, Ashraf remembers them all in a manner reminiscent of my grandfather's mental catalogue of food prices from the 1930s. Such information is important for a man who spends his idle hours thinking of trains to jump on to.

What about tickets?

'You don't need tickets. If the checker doesn't come, you travel for free. If you get caught, you simply go to jail.' Jail, according to Ashraf—who has never been to one—is an acceptable way of spending three months of a life in exchange for a short train ride. 'They don't make you work if you are in for less than six months,' he claims. 'All you do is eat and roam the premises.'

His audience at Kaka's tea shop is unconvinced. 'You have to drink from the same tap that you use to wash your latrine!' bellows Kaka, whose face, I have just realized, has acquired a crimson hue after years of sitting next to a lit stove. 'Have you ever drunk from a latrine?'

'Impossible!' Ashraf is aghast at the callousness of the state. 'Just last week the government distributed chlorine tablets worth ten thousand rupees at the chowk. For free! How can they make you drink from the latrine in jail?'

'They make you drink from the latrine,' Kaka insists as he throws a fistful of sugar into what looks like a pot full of liquid mud.

Ashraf retreats into a contemplative silence. He and I have arrived at a temporary truce regarding his past; I shall stop pestering him for details on the condition that he will bring them up himself at some point.

In the meantime, I look around for possible interview subjects. It is about six in the evening and we are sitting at Kaka's tea shop—again! Munna's story notwithstanding, I am bored of Bara Tooti and exhausted by its curious crowds, frustrated by their tendency to pick up my voice recorder and say 'Is this your mobile phone?' followed by 'So everything I say is being recorded?'

Yes, it is! Not only is it being recorded, I will be forced to listen to it when I review my tapes, forced to transcribe it in the hope that someone would have said something memorable, and forced to relive this moment when I review my transcripts. Over the last few months, my tapes are full of conversations just like these. In some I am ineffectually explaining how it doesn't have a tape but it can be converted into a CD; elsewhere I concede that though the paanwallah has a cellphone that doubles up as a recorder, my phone does not record and my recorder cannot phone. 'It's like using a saw to hammer a nail,' I point out rather brightly in one transcript.

'Ashraf bhai, can we please go somewhere else? I cannot have another cup of this tea.'

'What's wrong with the tea?'

'It's too sweet.'

'True. Kaka, your tea is bakwaas. Aman bhai says it's too sweet.'

'It's because of you bhenchods. All day long you chootiyas smoke ganja and then complain that the chai is pheeka! So I put more sugar, and then Aman bhai says it's too sweet, then Rehaan says it's expensive, then Lalloo says there isn't enough milk and you, you gaandu, say, "This time make mine special." No chai for anyone today!'

'Araam se, Kaka. I'm sorry.' I smile my best 'I'm one of the boys, but not really' smile.

'We could go to Kalyani's,' Ashraf suggests.

'What's Kalyani's?'

'It's a bit like...it's a bit like a permit room but without a permit.'

'You mean an illegal bar?' As a law-abiding denizen of South Delhi, I am instantly and constantly impressed by the illegality and ingenuity of the North. Having dismissed Ashraf's concerns about money with an imperious wave of my hand, we are finally off on an adventure into the depths of Sadar Bazaar. Well, at least I am; Ashraf just wants to get drunk.

We head down towards Teli Bara Road, past several buildings that I once romantically assumed were ruined havelis but which turned out to be perfectly functioning godowns. On my right I notice a small cinema ('Must watch a film in the hall,' say my notes from that day).

'Do you watch films, Ashraf bhai?'

'No.'

'Why?'

'No interest.'

Buoyed by the prospect of a drink at Kalyani's, Ashraf prattles on about the government as we walk through the market. Having dispensed with the railways, he is now telling me about the Delhi Excise Department, a department he often thinks about.

'I don't understand it,' he declares. 'See, Sheila Dikshit knows that there are homeless people in Delhi. How do we know that Sheila knows? Because every winter, the Delhi government sets up shaadi-style shamiana tents in Sadar Bazaar for mazdoors to sleep in. For free! Why would people leave their homes to sleep in a shamiana? They won't. Which means the sarkar knows that mazdoors are homeless.

'Now consider the Head of Excise. He knows that there is homelessness, he also knows that full ninety per cent of Delhi's desi sharab is sold in Sadar Bazaar area—the *same* area where Sheila puts up shelters for the homeless! What does this mean, Aman bhai?'

'It means these people drink themselves out of house and home?'

'No! Don't make a joke of this, everyone knows that isn't true. They drink it in the streets! So the Excise Department is making us break the rule! Otherwise they should just not sell it!'

'Would you prefer they didn't?'

'No, no,' Ashraf backtracked in some haste. 'I'm just saying I don't understand it.'

'Neither do I, Ashraf bhai.'

Drinking on the street is fun occasionally, but it loses colour really fast. Everyone is just a little bit nervous and so ends up drinking much faster than they would like to. Most mazdoors simply knock the bottle back in quick gulps and then wander about Bara Tooti in a daze. After seven, the chowk has a different feel to it—a rough edge exposed by the alcohol. A few fights break out, people intervene, and then the police show up.

The last time we drank out on the pavement, Ashraf almost got us both beaten up and arrested. The evening had started pleasantly enough—Ashraf and Lalloo were drinking quarters of the Mafia brand—Everyday, the chowk favourite, was not available and Shokeen, Ashraf's 'number two favourite', was sold out for the day—I was nursing a small drink myself, while Rehaan was telling us about the time an outbreak of the Ranikhet disease at his farm back home had forced him to kill off his entire flock of chickens. 'I grabbed each bird by the neck and forced a shot of rum down its throat. They ran around for a few minutes and then suddenly they became very still.'

'How did you know they were dead?' I asked. 'Maybe the alcohol just knocked them out.'

'That's exactly what it did. So then I dug a deep hole and buried them.'

'Alive?'

'Well, asleep. Buried them asleep,' said Rehaan, folding his hands under his head like a pillow as if to emphasize the humanity of this avian genocide.

Thwack! A steel-tipped lathi struck the bottle of Mafia

with inch-perfect accuracy, scattering shards of glass across the pavement. We looked up to see a giant policeman glowering at us, his stick poised for another strike.

'Bhenchodon! Who said you could drink on this pavement? Go drink in your house!'

'Where else can we drink, Constable saab? The chowk is our house; this pavement is our drawing room.' Ashraf had been drinking since six.

'Chootiya, I'll make the police station your bedroom if you don't shut up right now. What's under that shawl?' Whack, whack, whack—the lathi struck the pavement on either side of Lalloo.

'Police saab, we made a mistake, forgive us, forgive us, forgive us.' Lalloo stretched out on the pavement, his hands alternately touching the constable's shoes and covering his own head to ward off further blows.

'And you? Who are you? Who are you?' The lathi waved in my direction.

'He's from the press!'

Thanks, Ashraf, why don't you give him my home address and telephone number as well.

'What are you doing here? Encouraging this sort of illegal behaviour?'

'He is from the press; he can go wherever he wants!' It was Ashraf again. He was talking too much now. 'Whenever he wants! However he wants.' Shut up, Ashraf, shut up! Please just shut up!

'I am interviewing them, officerji,' I explained, standing up and adopting what I hoped was a professorial air. 'This is an important part of my research.'

It took another fifteen minutes to resolve the matter, with no help from Mohammed Ashraf who piped up every time the constable showed signs of calming down. 'You tell us where to drink! Should we drink in your thana then? I'll come every day at six o'clock.'

Fortunately, Rehaan and Lalloo shut him up. I smoothened the constable's ruffled feathers and sent him on his way. 'I'm warning you,' he said as he walked off. 'Don't mix with this lot. There is a cell waiting for them in the lock-up—you'll get thrown in as well.'

Ashraf was incandescent. 'Why didn't you flash your press card and tell him to fuck off?'

'Oh really? What was I supposed to tell him? "Hi, I'm from the press, so why don't you fuck off while I break the law and drink in the open with my friends?"'

'All of you are the same. In front of the police, tumhari phat jaati hai—you get fucked!'

'Shut up, Ashraf, I'm going home.'

•

It is to escape the tyrannies of the officials of the Excise Department and the evil henchmen in the Delhi Police that Ashraf now leads me to 'a secret place that everyone knows'. Somewhere in Sadar Bazaar, a low-slung tarpaulin worm sprawls lazily along the footpath. From a distance it appears to be a consignment of material waiting to be loaded onto an arriving truck but on closer examination reveals itself as a tunnel-like hut fronted entirely by interlocking sheets of cardboard and ply. At one end, a heavy wooden blanket masks a sturdy wooden door on which Ashraf now gently knocks. 'This is Kalyani's—the secret place,' he says. 'Don't mention the location in your book.'

Originally a series of individual rooms divided by thatch and plywood partitions, the structure has since had its inner walls knocked down to create a hall about twenty feet long and about seven feet high. While the road-facing wall of Kalyani's is an impregnable assemblage of wood, cardboard, and tarpaulin, the far wall has been folded up, offering much-needed ventilation and a pleasing view of a set of railway tracks. 'This is Kalyani's,' begins Ashraf somewhat unnecessarily, 'and that is Kalyani.'

'Ashraf,' Kalyani greets him with genuine enthusiasm even as she appraises me with some suspicion. She puts her head to one side and stares at me like an annoyed hen, an impression heightened by her sharp nose, her light, bobbing gait, and her dark hair pulled back into a tight bun that sits high on her almost perfectly spherical head. She is slender, about thirty-five years old, and speaks, like Ashraf, with a soft Bihari accent. 'This is Aman bhai. He's a friend of mine—he is okay.'

'Whatever you say, Ashraf.' She pours him a steep glass of Everyday. 'Does he drink?' For a second I hesitate, only to be revisited by the memory of an Everyday hangover that felt like a kick to the head, and politely refuse. She gives me a look of pity with just a trace of contempt and hands me a handful of raisins. 'Chaba le,' she says caustically, as she slips out through a fold in the wall.

As I chew on raisins, Ashraf goes about finishing his half bottle of Everyday. Made from the finest commonly available ingredients, Everyday whisky isn't for everyone. New recruits often shun this intoxicating brew, in favour of more bombastic brands like Hulchul that shakes the very foundations of a man's being; Jalwa Spiced Country Liquor that speaks of youth, fire, and passion; Toofan, infused with the pent-up vigour and vitality of an impending storm; and Ghadar Desi that is a perfect antidote to colonial oppression.

Enclosed in a squarish, clear-glass bottle, the name printed across in simple bilingual lettering, Everyday makes no such promises, its prosaic name serving as a reminder of an incontrovertible truth: Everyday—for those who crave it every day, day after day.

The best way to drink Everyday is to mix about two inches of the liquor with half an inch of water and knock it back in largish gulps. The first sip is usually the worst. The raw, metallic taste of uncured alcohol bites down on the tongue like a steel clamp, inducing an almost irrepressible urge to spit out the offending liquid. However, once the gag reflex has been suppressed, each sip becomes successively easier till the taste becomes irrelevant. Veterans recommend that each glass be accompanied by light stomach liners like hard-boiled eggs, a plate of raw paneer, and a plentiful supply of Howrah beedis.

After enough Everyday, Tilak Bridge looks like Howrah Bridge, Sadar Bazaar looks like Bara Bazaar, India Gate looks like the Gateway of India. After enough Everyday, Lalloo looks like Kaka, Rehaan looks like Munna, house painters look like lost artists, carpenters seem as sombre as Supreme Court judges. The broad intersections of the bazaar divide into the side streets of smaller towns. The tea shop on Barna Galli becomes Bhisu da's place in Tangra, the butcher up the street in Kasaipura becomes the halal shop in Malad. After enough Everyday, Mohammed Ashraf occasionally drops his guard and talks about what's really bothering him.

Today he is feeling bored, even depressed, by the chowk, his life, everything. 'I have no friends here,' he says. 'In Dilli there is azadi, but there is also a lot of akelapan, the loneliness of being a stranger in every city. Har sheher mein ajnabi.'

'But what about Lalloo? Isn't Lalloo your friend?'

'He is, but he isn't a jigri yaar. He isn't my close friend.'

'What sort of friend is he?'

'He is a medium-type friend.'

This is another of Ashraf's terms—medium-type. Classification is important to Ashraf: it is important to draw lines, make tables, and, most essentially, mark time. To distinguish between now and then, yesterday and today, because tomorrow and thereafter may be better or worse or at least different. Marking time is important as it allows for planning. Planning is crucial, as it indicates a degree of purpose without which a man could easily lose his way. Bara Tooti is full of those who, according to Ashraf, have lost their way; and in the presence of such company, it is important to run on his own sense of time.

The passing of time is rarely a matter of comment at Bara Tooti. For most regulars time is measured as the distance between the point when the bus fare from Moradabad to Delhi was four rupees, dehadi was eighteen rupees, and a room at Takiya Wali Masjid could be rented for twelve rupees a month, to now when the rents have risen to three hundred rupees a month, dehadi is a hundred and fifty rupees and the bus ticket is a hundred and twelve rupees.

For Lalloo, entire weeks run into each other before he senses their passing. Most events occur either too fast to register, or too slowly to notice. Lalloo doesn't even know how long it has been since he came to Delhi, since he went home, since he last spoke to his wife. Yes, Lalloo has a wife, in a house on the Nepal border in faraway Gorakhpur. I found out by accident, when Lalloo and Ashraf were once particularly drunk. 'Take down his story, Aman bhai, he even has a wife,' Ashraf exclaimed. 'And a father-in-law who is a big man in the coal mining business.'

But Lalloo was too drunk to talk that day and the next time, it was as if the conversation had never occurred. 'What wife, Aman bhai? What father-in-law? What coal mine? You have been observing us all this time. Where would I hide her?'

With the exception of Ashraf, no one at the chowk makes the effort of talking to me more than they have to. There is a point when even a good chat can stop being time-pass and become a chore—particularly a chat that doesn't respect the careful conventions of place and time.

Chowk time creeps along at its own glacial pace, marked only by epochal events and the coming and going of regulars: the year of Indira Gandhi's assassination, the year of Kale Baba's first illness, the year of Lambu Mistry's return. Seasons will change, and Ashraf and Lalloo will move cyclically around the lamp post with the surveillance cameras. In summer they will sit in the northwest quadrant of the chowk, shielded from the blazing sun. In winter they will shift to the centre to soak in the sun's comforting warmth. In the monsoons, they can sleep in the southeast quadrant, where the sheltered pavements offer respite from the rains.

Occasionally events can shake the chowk out of its monotony, alerting its residents to the transformations around them. In one particularly fast-paced year, even as dehadi remained constant, Kaka raised the price of tea three times, citing the rising prices of sugar and milk, thus forcing his patrons to work harder for longer hours. In another year, before Ashraf's time, three regulars died of pneumonia, making it seem like the winter lasted right up to April when the last old-timer finally succumbed to his illness.

For Ashraf, a stable friendship is premised on a shared notion of time. When Ashraf describes his childhood friends, for instance, he speaks of a group that woke up together, skipped class together, and felt hungry, thirsty, horny, lonesome, and depressed in the perfect synchronicity of 'close friends'. Twenty years later, each one has different scales of time by which they weigh the importance of each passing moment: some are district collectors for whom the clock ticks each time the state government changes; others, now policemen, set their watches to the length of the commissioner's tenure. Still others have become businessmen who mark time in the days it takes for their payments to arrive, while Ashraf waits on a footpath in Delhi, making medium-term plans with medium-type friends.

'Medium-type friends are those who do not make chootiyas of each other. If I ask you to help me out, it is expected that you will, on the condition I actually need your help and am not asking you simply because I'm too lazy to help myself. And the same goes for when you need help. And even then, you won't give me assistance. You'll *lend* it to me. Get it? You'll *lend* it; and I'll *return* it. So it's contractual. Dehadi friendship, that's what it is—dehadi friendship where everything is out in the open and no one is making a chootiya out of anyone.

'I need to get out of this city, Aman bhai; here I am in very bad company—sangat hi kharaab hai. I need to go to a city like Calcutta where even the dehadi mazdoors are family-type people, who come to work and then go home to sleep with their wives and kids... I mean they don't sleep with their kids but you know what I mean...' On and on Ashraf chatters.

'I'm telling you, no fighting-shightng, no daaru-shaaru, no gaali-galoch, no randi-baazi...'

I really should be noting all of this down, but I am more interested in Kalyani. 'No cursing-shursing, choda-chodi, jhagda-shagda...' Even as Ashraf natters on, she bustles about—sometimes picking up one of the many children who clatter around the back of the room, sometimes giving Ashraf some water. At least ten different people come in, stare at me, talk to her in surreptitious whispers, and slip out silently. Still, Ashraf talks on...

When he finally concludes, I ask him if I can interview Kalyani.

'Why?' He appears annoyed that his life is not exciting enough to be the sole subject of my research.

'Because she is the first woman I have met in Sadar.'

It's not as if there aren't any women in North Delhi—I have seen them on buses on the Ring Road, along the riverbank near what used to be Yamuna Pushta working class residential colony before it was demolished by the Municipal Corporation, in tiny tea shops in the mohallas of what used to be Sanjay Amar Colony before it was demolished by the corporation, in Nangla Maachi before it was demolished by the corporation, in LNJP before it was demolished by the corporation, and of course near the railway station. So they clearly exist; but not here in Sadar Bazaar. In Sadar, all the chaiwallahs are men, the waiters are men, the beedi sellers are men; the pavements are littered with male vegetable sellers, male jewellery salesmen, male tailors, and male cooks. Even the sari and blouse salespersons are men.

But Kalyani is undeniably a woman. 'Not just any woman, Aman bhai, she is a business-type woman.'

'You can ask her, but she will ninety per cent say no,' says Ashraf with a surety that borders on smugness.

I ask Kalyani if I can interview her.

She says no.

Ashraf laughs to himself.

'I'll tell you her story, don't worry.' The whisky has made him magnanimous. 'Kalyani has two businesses—daana and daaru.'

2

'Side, side, side.' The crowds looked up at the giant trucks tiptoeing along Naya Bazaar's narrow gallis and obligingly 'gave side'. It was three in the afternoon; the trucks weren't supposed be here—they were allowed to enter the city only between 8 pm and 8 am. But the grain merchants of Naya Bazaar worked twenty-four hours a day: the police had been paid off, and business continued as it must. The police kept an eye on every truck that entered—each consignment meant a commission. The truck drivers kept an eye out for policemen—they had been given an exact amount of money for the cops; what they saved, they kept.

As soon as one truck pulled into the godown, it was set upon on all sides by a swarm of workers armed with vicious steel hooks that they used as handles to gain purchase on the soft gunny sacks. A chain was formed with two loaders frantically hacking at the cargo with their hooks and tossing the sacks down to an assembly line of palledars who carried the load into the godown. A foreman rushed about exhorting his team to unload before the police arrived. 'Jaldi, jaldi, jaldi,' he screamed, even as the hooks bit into the sacks' soft flesh, scattering showers of grain. 'Careful, careful, you chootiyas,' he cautioned. 'Don't damage the goods.'

The driver gunned the engine even as the last bag of rice was thrown off, and the truck shouldered its way out of the market as quickly as it could.

As the truck left, a young woman emerged from a corner of the courtyard, darted across the parking bay, and swept up the mixture of grain, mud, and grit into a gunny sack in one smooth motion. Before anyone could react, she had slung the bag over her shoulder and disappeared into the jostling streets.

●

The first time she did it, it took Kalyani three days to sift through that one sack of grain and grit, from which she got three kilos of clean, fragrant basmati rice. A few months later, she was collecting between ten and fifteen kilos of rice a day which she sold every Wednesday at the weekly market on Koria Pull.

She was careful not to visit the same godown too often, but word invariably got around. The same team of palledars moved from godown to godown and spread the news of a fleet-footed young woman who had discovered yet another way to make an honest day's living in Sadar Bazaar. The workers called her 'chidiya'—the little bird who scratched around for grain and flew off when anyone approached. As her business grew, she slowly began hiring women from across the basti and paid them to clean the rice. A year later, Kalyani approached the godown owners in Naya Bazaar and offered them a flat fee for the right to collect rice, wheat, and pulses from their premises. Once the owners agreed, she hired a group of women to work as grain collectors—and prepared to get rich.

'It's all about control. To run a business you need control—over yourself. Kalyani has control. She spends the whole day in a house full of liquor. Can you imagine me doing that?'

Frankly, I can't. I can't imagine Ashraf spending more than five minutes in the proximity of a bottle before draining it.

'See, that's what I mean. Even with a business-type brain you need a control-type personality. Now look at Kalyani, and look at me.

'Kalyani is always looking for ways to make money: that's her personality. So am I, but I'm a mast maula, dil chowda, seena sandook, lowda bandook! A dancing adventurer, with my heart for a treasure chest and my penis for a gun.

'People like us never have any money. The moment we earn some, we give to someone like Kalyani.'

Since the daana business now runs itself, Kalyani devotes a lot of her time to the daaru business—it's much less work and the margins are much higher. The shack where we are sitting is a relatively new space; Kalyani moved in about a year and a half ago, after her house on the Yamuna bank was demolished as part of a slum clearance drive ordered by the Delhi High Court. The family moved to Sadar to be closer to her business and found a place right opposite a desi sharab theka.

Liquor vends in Delhi fall under two separate excise categories: L-2 licences meant for 'English Wine and

Beer' shops that stock 'Indian made foreign liquor' like whisky, beer, rum, or vodka, and L-10 licences for desi sharab shops that stock country-made liquor like Hulchul, Toofan, and Mafia. This may seem a minor difference, but wine and beer shops are authorized to open at noon, while desi sharab thekas can only open after five in the evening. The idea is to discourage Delhi's working class from drinking on the job, but instead, the policy forces drinkers like Ashraf to buy higher priced 'English wine' through the day before shifting to desi sharab after five.

It didn't take long for Kalyani to spot the need for an off-hours desi sharab vend. One evening, she took some money out of her daana business and sent her husband to buy a crate of desi sharab at twenty-five rupees a quarter bottle and sold it the next day for thirty-five rupees a quarter bottle. It was more expensive than a licensed vendor, but cheaper than the English Wine and Beer shops.

Soon patrons began to arrive at all times of the day. Loaders, having loaded their trucks in time for the border closing at eight in the morning, showed up at nine and stayed till noon. Painters, like Ashraf, slathered on a layer of primer and stopped by for a drink while they waited for the foundation layers to dry. Through the day, Kalyani continued with her various other engagements: her clients entered and left from the daaru end of the tunnel, while her grain sorters used the daana entrance at the other end.

After a while, workers at Bara Tooti began coming to her during regular hours, even though Kalyani's was much more expensive. Almost by accident, Kalyani had set up Bara Tooti's first bar where mazdoors, beldaars, and mistrys could gather through the day, swap stories, and settle contracts over a few drinks.

On still summer evenings, when the oppressive closeness of the jhuggi became impossible to bear, she would roll up one entire side of the tent so that patrons could watch trains as they shunted up and down the railway tracks. On winter nights, the crowded shack exuded the warm, cosy glow of whisky and company.

Soon Kalyani cut a deal with the local liquor vend to supply to her in bulk amounts and came to an agreement with the local policemen. Kalyani was an ardent supporter of the Delhi Police—law enforcement was necessary for a favourable investment climate. If the police didn't harass people drinking on the streets, why would people come to Kalyani's?

'We wouldn't. Well, maybe I would, because Kalyani is now a friend, but ninety per cent people would not come.'

'What sort of friend is she, Ashraf bhai?'

'No, Aman bhai, she is a married woman—shaadi-shuda. She also has kids—three of them!'

'So? Maybe she secretly despises her husband and wants to leave him.'

'No, she doesn't. I have met him several times.'

'Well, I don't think you should let that stop you. I think she is a great girl.'

'In that case I think you should fuck her. Just show her your press card; I'm sure that would impress her.'

Ashraf continues to protest vehemently, but I am convinced that he should try his luck with Kalyani; if nothing else, at least for the sake of my story. Looking back at my notes, I find I have been needlessly sensitive about certain issues—primarily sex. There is no sex in my story—a lacuna that could easily be addressed if Ashraf has some.

Ashraf is at least in his late thirties. Does he not have sex?

'In Dilli? No. Absolutely not. No chance, never. Ekdum NO.' Rarely have I seen Ashraf exhibit a resolve so steady. So has he ever had sex at all?

'Of course. Multiple times on several occasions. Just not in Dilli, it's not safe. I know these things. I once whitewashed a chodai khana on GB Road; there I saw everything. Some poor chootiya will ask, "Kitna?" and the randi will assure him, "Hundred rupees," or something. But once he's in, they will take everything he has. Everything—watch, belt, rings, money, everything! And you can't even report these people to the police.'

'Why?'

'Why? Because then you'll go straight from the chodai khana into the police thana, Aman bhai, and it's hard to tell which is worse.'

'So what's a good place?'

'Bombay. Calcutta is not bad, but Bombay is the best. Kamatipura. Get off at Grant Road Railway Station, walk towards Bhindi Bazaar. My favourite was this girl in Arab Galli—her father walked with a limp. I visited her every Tuesday and paid between fifty and a hundred rupees depending on her mood.'

'When were you in Bombay?'

'Many years ago, before I came here.'

'Why Tuesday?'

'Tuesday means half day at the shop.'

'What shop?'

'The meat shop where I worked.'

'What was her name?'

'I don't know, Aman bhai—it's not like I was marrying her.'

3

'PHAAT! On the cheek! On my cheek, he pasted one. Phaat.'
Arm pulled back past his shoulder Ashraf mimics the action, a
crisp straight-elbowed arc that almost lands on my cheek.

If every city that Ashraf has visited has had a single
defining moment, then in Bombay, that moment is 'the slap'.

'It was like "Phaat", not two quick phut-phut-type smacks.
No, it was a chaanta—phataack.'

We are still drinking at Kalyani's. I have finished my
raisins and, to Kalyani's relief, have poured myself a large
drink. 'She gets nervous when people don't drink,' Ashraf
says, as he warms to his tale.

To deflect my queries about his sex life, Ashraf has offered
me what he thinks might be a comparable anecdote about
his time in Bombay—this being the first I have heard of him
having lived in that city. I am still trying to build a year-wise
timeline of Ashraf's life but as far as Ashraf is concerned, he
was brought up in Patna and is now in Delhi—everything

else can only be accessed via oblique enquiries. As a result, every interview is a bit like playing a word association game. Kalyani to sex to Bombay whorehouse to slapping.

'You got slapped in a whorehouse, Ashraf bhai?' I'm laughing through the fixed grimace I acquire when exposed to desi alcohol.

'No, yaar. Not in the whorehouse, in the meat shop. Kuch ho gaya tha. Something happened.'

Up to this point, I had assumed that the meat shop *was* the whorehouse, but I'm clearly mistaken.

'Kya ho gaya? What happened? Where were you? Tell me from the beginning.'

'That's what I'm doing—so I get off the train...'

'Why were you on the train, where were you going?'

'Aman bhai...'

'Arre, at least tell me the basic facts.'

'You take the mazaa out of every story. Where's your glass? Oye Kalyani, where's Aman bhai's glass? Pour another one for Aman bhai.'

●

Submerged in the depths of a train compartment, a slender figure struggled through the crush of commuters on the Monday morning Virar Slow. As the train pulled into Malad Station Mohammed Ashraf burst through the crowd and scurried down the road.

Late night, last night—kuch ho gaya, kuch ho gaya. He can explain, they will understand, something happened, some things happen.

Slip, trip, jump, slide—the long road past the church had never looked so long. Up the slope, up the slope, almost there, almost there, panting, gasping, 'Salaam walekum, Maalik.'

'That's when he slapped me. In front of everyone.'

'Phaaat!' Onomatopoeia is one of Ashraf's many talents.

'A slap like that, Aman bhai, that's a full stop. Once you get slapped like that in front of everyone, you can never work in there again. Your izzat is gone; no one will ever give you respect, and a head kasai cannot function without respect.'

The story started with Mohammed Ashraf installed as the head kasai of Fauji Halal Shop in Malad whose proprietor was a Javed Qureshi.

The head kasai decides everything: who does what, who sits where, and also other things like when the knives should be changed, how often the floor should be mopped. In a chicken shop, the floor must always be clean. If the floor is clean, the customer will think everything is clean. All these things must be decided in advance because once the day begins, there is no time.

Apart from cleanliness, the other important thing is speed. The head kasai sets the speed of the shop. Speed is crucial—the more time a customer spends in a shop, the dirtier he is likely to think it is. The customer is like a child; he must be distracted immediately. The kasai should grab the chicken and keep asking questions—'Is it for curry? Or kebabs?', 'Big pieces or small?', 'Do you want the liver?'—all to keep the customer engrossed. Once the customer's attention starts to wander, he will stare closely at the kasai's hands, he will wonder how often the kasai washes them, he may notice the fly buzzing around inside the glass display case, maybe a cockroach will run across the floor. By the time he gets his chicken, he will be so full of sights, sounds, and smells that he may never return to the shop again.

In a fast shop, the head kasai is like a hungry machine: shredding, cutting, slicing, and chopping everything that is placed before him. His assistants function like boiler room boys—shovelling fuel so that the furnace never goes cold. Customers step up to the cage and pick their chicken; the assistant tags the chicken with a plastic counter, beheads it quickly and cleanly, and flings it into the dibba to cool down. The kasai reaches in, pulls out the chicken, calls out the number, asks the customer how he wants it cut, and hands over the cut bird—all in less than ten minutes.

'In full form, I could skin, cut, clean, and dice a whole chicken in about two minutes. I had studied biology up to first year college so I knew exactly how to cut the bird. I only had to learn to undress the chicken, which is easy once you know the basic technique.'

'What's that, Ashraf bhai?'

'Kapde utarna, Aman bhai, the technique for undressing is always the same—be it a goat, a bird, or a woman. Start from the limbs and work your way inwards and upwards. Make cuts near the legs, tear the skin away from each side, and then reach up to the neck and peel from the head downwards.

'Once I had perfected my skinning technique, it was only a matter of time before I became a head kasai. No one else in the shop had my kind of skill.' Ashraf reaches out for the Everyday to replenish his glass and mine. 'You will not believe me, Aman bhai. I was a brilliant kasai—one of the best in Bombay. I could make one kilo of chicken into one and a half kilos simply by skinning it.'

The trick, as I learnt later, is fairly common among most experienced butchers. It takes a while to master, but once learnt—like any good conjuring trick—it is impossible for the audience to spot.

'The first step is to strip the chicken of its feathers and skin it as carefully as you can. Then dip it in the rinsing tub and wash it thoroughly. Now, everyone washes the chicken; but before washing make two deep incisions just above the thigh, where the leg joins the abdomen, and make sure the water is slightly warm. Then you knead the chicken legs in a smooth pumping action—pumping is crucial—and the flesh soaks up the water just like a sponge. It only takes a few seconds, while the customer stands there marvelling at the time you have taken to wash his chicken. By the time you cut it, the chicken will look pinker, firmer, healthier, and even its head will swell up to twice its size. The customer will be happy with the juicy, healthy chicken, your maalik will be happy with the extra money, and you will be happy because he will make you head kasai.'

'So what happened that day, Ashraf bhai?'

'That's what I'm coming to. Listen.

'One Saturday, maybe six months after I became the head kasai, I went out somewhere with my friends. We had a few drinks, it got very late, and I couldn't make it back to the shop the next day. Sunday is always the busiest day of the week; in Bombay, the day when the menfolk buy the meat for the house. The women will buy the vegetables, but the men buy the meat. It is the only thing they buy—and Sunday everyone has a holiday from office.'

That day, the queue stretched from the entrance of the shop all the way to the church down the road. Ashraf estimates that Qureshi, the owner, lost between five and seven thousand rupees that day. 'Easily, kum se kum. Not to mention what it would take to win back all the business he lost that day.

'So when I arrived on Monday—that too ten minutes late, he slapped me—full on the face, in front of everyone... and bas, it was over. I turned around and never went back to the shop again.'

'You could have waited for his temper to cool and then gone back, no?'

'I could. But I didn't.'

'Why?'

'This is temporary kaam, Aman bhai. If my heart is in it, I will say sorry and listen to the maalik's insults and take his blows and slaps. But when my heart isn't in it? I won't. The maalik owns my work, Aman bhai, he doesn't own me. Who is he to slap anyone? And what will I get with his forgiveness?'

'Your job for one, Ashraf bhai.'

'I don't need a job like that.'

'So then?'

'So then I left Bombay. Once I had left Patna—I left my mother, my brother, my cousins, my friends, my life—what was the difference between Delhi and Bombay? Bombay and Calcutta? I didn't leave my home to get slapped by someone like that, Aman bhai.'

'So why did you leave home, Ashraf bhai?'

'That's a story for another day. I did some mazdoor work in Bombay for a few days, then someone told me there was lots of work in Delhi. So I took a train to Surat, and from there to Punjab. I spent a month in Haryana and then one day I showed up at Old Delhi Railway Station.'

'So what did you do when you came here?'

'I met a bunch of chootiyas at Bara Tooti.'

'Kalyaaaaniii, can we have some more?' And the bottle of Everyday continued its dizzying orbit.

•

'Why are you doing this, Aman bhai?' Ashraf wonders as we stumble cross-eyed through Teli Bara.

'Doing what, Ashraf bhai?'

'Why are you spending all this time and money getting drunk with lafunters like us? What can we teach you?'

'I'm trying to write a book.'

'But who will want to read it?'

'I don't know. I suppose my friends will buy it and maybe a few people interested in Delhi.'

'But will you make any money?'

'Well, I've already made some money.'

'How much money?'

'Enough to buy a laptop.'

'Oh good.' Relieved that I, like everyone else, have found a way to make just enough money off Sadar Bazaar, Ashraf stops at a tiny roadside shrine under a tree. 'Mata ki kasam, Aman bhai, you will make lots of money.'

'So will you, Ashraf bhai.'

'And Lalloo—even if he is only my medium-type friend, he is my only friend, Aman bhai. My only friend. And Rehaan too.'

'And Kaka too.'

'We will all be rich, Aman bhai.'

'Yes, Ashraf, some day we will all be rich.'

4

The morning after the drunken night at Kalyani's I have decided it is finally time to sit down with Ashraf and sketch out a timeline of his life. I have a vague idea of the major events, but not a clear sense of the arc of his life. I've looked back at my notes and the years don't seem to add up. Either Ashraf is only thirty years old, or there is a considerable chunk of his life still missing. This will be a no-holds-barred interview where no subject would be too sensitive or personal.

My efforts are complicated by the fact that this morning, Ashraf is drunk. Not drunk-drunk in the unsteady, slurring, and hiccuping fashion, but drunk in an organized and matter-of-fact way—the sort of drunkeness that comes at the end of a cycle he once described to me in his meticulous fashion.

It goes something like this:

Time: 6 pm
Money: About three hundred rupees between the two of them.

Ashraf and Lalloo have just finished work. The shop's bright pink, still-wet walls have the velvety texture of a wedding cake. The shopkeeper is happy with their work. He has paid them without complaint.

The desi sharab shop is open for business. Ashraf and Lalloo buy a half each of Everyday for fifty rupees apiece, and another quarter each for twenty-five rupees apiece.

Time: 11 pm
Money: About one hundred rupees

The half bottles are over. Fifty rupees have been spent on something, but on what exactly? Ashraf isn't sure. There was some food—boiled eggs, maybe a roti or two? With dal. If there was roti, there must have been dal. Possibly a cup of tea. Six rupees were spent on squishy packets of water—that is certain.

The pauwas, or quarter bottles, are still intact; Ashraf keeps them in his breast pocket. He keeps the money in his shoes. He wraps his shoes in his pants. He puts his pants under his head—like a pillow. He throws a shawl over himself.

Time: 2 am, maybe later
Money: Indeterminate

The fever-like hold of Everyday breaks. Ashraf wakes up with a start. He is sweating profusely. He is desperately thirsty. He staggers across to a leaky tap down the road and drinks in long, deep gulps. He returns to his spot to find Lalloo awake and in a similar state. It's impossible to sleep; the flickering street lamp gives Ashraf a headache. He can feel the pavement tremble below him. Somewhere underground, something is stirring. Is the Metro still under construction?

Lalloo suggests they crack open one of the quarter bottles. Ashraf agrees. Half an hour later, they have finished both bottles. Sleep arrives with the suddenness of a road accident.

Time: 7:30 am

Money: Twenty rupees

Some maderchod has stolen the money. Lalloo still has some left, but Ashraf's shoes have been picked clean. Ashraf is sick. The alcohol has made him woozy. Kaka is sympathetic, he offers them tea on credit. They meet Rehaan at the tea shop. Rehaan has another twenty rupees. The thekas haven't opened yet; it's way too early. They walk down to Kalyani's. She takes thirty-five rupees and gives them only a quarter to split between them. Her tea is free, though.

Time: 9:30 am

Money: Five rupees

Five rupees buys two rotis and some dal. They now have no money at all. They sit at the chowk trying to look sober and employable. Ashraf has brought out the lucky charm that he saves for situations like this: the condom, or 'kandome' as he calls it.

The kandome is a broad, heavy brush with long, thick bristles encrusted with paint. The bright red handle is solid wood and fits just right. It is the most useless brush Ashraf owns: it's too heavy and soaks up too much paint.

'I bought it when I was just starting out. It looks like a brush a professional would use.'

A well-stocked bag is a sign of tajurba, experience. A maalik likes a workman with impressive-looking tools. At the chowk, where safediwallahs are arranged like mannequins in a shop window, the maalik is drawn to the one with five, six, seven, brushes in his bag. He thinks this man is a true karigar; he has a different brush for each surface. It's not a brush, it's a badge of honour.

'It's just like a kandome, Aman bhai. On TV you may stand next to Shabana Azmi and promise to use it, but you know you never will.'

Time: 1:30 pm
Money: Hundred rupees

The kandome has protected them. They are lucky to have found this job—a small shop beyond Mithai Pull towards Baraf Khana. It is lunchtime, the maalik has agreed to give them fifty rupees each for lunch. He will deduct it from the money he will pay them in the evening. A plate of chana kulcha each sets them back ten rupees. The desi sharab theka is still shut: it opens only at five. But the English store has been open for an hour and a half; it doesn't keep Everyday, so they settle for rum at seventy rupees for an addha.

Time: 6 pm
Money: Two hundred and twenty rupees

Ashraf and Lalloo have just finished work. The desi sharab theka is open for business.

Ashraf's appetite for work and alcohol varies inversely. The more he works, the less he drinks; he eats better, his face fills out, he gets his salt-and-pepper hair coloured boot-polish black, and he spouts irreverent verses. This virtuous feedback loop continues till work runs out, at which point Ashraf and Lalloo drink away the money they have saved over weeks of work. Ashraf's cheeks start to hollow, he stops shaving, the hair dye fades away.

Today, his hands are trembling and his hair looks like it has been trimmed with garden shears.

'At what point in the cycle are you now, Ashraf bhai?'

'I don't know, Aman bhai. But you ask your questions, don't worry.' Ashraf rubs his temples; he really does look very sick, but I am determined to chalk out the timeline. It is unlikely that Ashraf will work today; it takes at least a day to recover from this sort of drinking, so I might as well use this time.

'When did you get to Delhi, Ashraf bhai?'

'Not sure, some years ago.'

'Which year—1999, 2000, 2001?'

'Which year is it now?'

'What are your earliest memories, Ashraf bhai? Do you remember any events—riots, floods, drought?'

'I remember, in school... I was quite senior then. I was cycling to Grace Ma'am's early one morning with the newspaper. Back then I could still read some English. Stopped outside her house. I remember handing her the paper—it was *The Times of India*, Patna edition—and her drowsiness giving way to sheer panic when she distractedly glanced at the headlines.

'Ashraf? What are you doing here? You must go home. You must go home!'

'Why, Grace Ma'am? Is there no school today?'

'Ashraf!' She was getting hysterical now. 'Go home. Go Home.'

'But why?'

She held up the paper. 'Indira is Dead!' 'Indira is dead!' She was shaking now, crying. 'Please go home. God knows what will happen. Indira is DEAD!'

Ashraf used to cycle down to Grace Ma'am's twice a day. Once in the mornings to drop off *The Times of India* and once in the evenings with the Hindi papers. She couldn't read the latter, which was half the problem. That, according to Ashraf, is when he became a 'complete harami'.

Grace Ma'am had a secret. She taught moral science and mathematics at a missionary school, but she played the lottery. She didn't smoke, or drink; she wasn't married, had no kids. She needed to do something, so she played lottery. Kalpataru—that was her favourite brand. Everyone has their own brands that they think are 'lucky' brands. But a lucky brand of lottery tickets is like a lucky pack of cigarettes—nonsense, all of it.

'Ashraf, put fifty rupees in Kalpataru,' she would say in her funny, slightly accented Hindi. She was a 'Madrasi from Kerala'. She was a nice lady, but never won anything. Ashraf used to sell her tickets anyway—he was a real business-type child. Early mornings he would sell boiled eggs and bread, in the day he would go to school, and in the afternoons he would buy lottery tickets for thirty paise each and sell them for fifty paise. As a kid, Ashraf always had money.

One day a gentleman-type lady came to his table and hurriedly asked for Kalpatru tickets. 'Jaldi, jaldi,' she said, and immediately he knew that she was scared. In those days, gentleman-type ladies couldn't buy lottery tickets, and certainly not schoolteachers. Grace Ma'am could have lost her job. So he said, 'I don't have enough tickets right now, I can drop them off at your house.' So that's how it started.

Every morning, he would go to her house to drop off the morning newspapers and in the afternoons—on days when the results were coming out—he would go with the Hindi newspapers. *The Times of India* never carried lottery results back then—at least not for Kalpatru brand.

'She would say, "One-rupee ticket: number nine, seven, five, whatever. Two-rupee tickets, five-rupee tickets..." Like that she would call out the numbers.'

He would look at the tickets and in front of her, with a straight face, without blinking, without sweating, calmly say, 'No, Grace Ma'am, nothing today, all the tickets are zero today.' She would just let the tickets drop to the floor, like she was worried the numbers would get stuck to her fingers. Ashraf would pick them up and claim the rewards.

'Even when she won?'

'Only when she won, Aman bhai. You can really be quite stupid sometimes. Sometimes I let her win. Sometimes when she had won five hundred rupees, I would say it was only two hundred rupees and keep the rest. It was a great business.' Ashraf is wistful, impressed by the derring-do of his younger self. 'Back then I was a true business-type.'

'And now?'

'Now I am a choosa hua aam, a mango sucked dry. Back then I could do anything. Anything! I once started a business worth lakhs with just fifty rupees!

'You will not believe me now, Aman bhai, but I used to be a major-level thekedar. Me and Raja, together we ran the biggest thekas in Raja Bazaar.'

'In Bombay?'

'No, no. In Calcutta. I was briefly in Calcutta before I went to Bombay. I was there for three years. I had uncles in Calcutta.'

'You never told me this.'

'I must have forgotten. I started a business with a friend of mine—a good, close friend—Raja. He was really smart.'

'The same guy who was a Double BA because he had two wives?'

'Same guy.'

5

Raja was so shrewd that he left his first wife and seduced and married a much older woman who owned not one, but two houses in the lanes of Raja Bazaar. So Raja never paid rent, and saved all his money.

Raja was so fair that when people asked him where he was from, he said 'Punjab' and they believed him. People automatically placed their trust in him. He had a noble bearing even though his father came from Bangladesh and named him after the marketplace where he was born—Raja from Raja Bazaar.

Before Ashraf met Raja, he was a normal dehadi-type. He worked twelve-hour shifts at the Royal Bengal Slipper Factory where he fitted leather foot straps onto sandal soles and dropped the finished product into a plastic bag. The owner was a bastard. He paid Ashraf fifteen rupees a day. In six months, Ashraf moved to Prince Footwear. Now he poured molten plastic into moulds to make plastic footwear. Plastic footwear was the height of fashion in Calcutta. Still is. Everybody wanted a pair. Ashraf made eighteen rupees a day.

Then Ashraf met Raja and became a business-type. In a sense, he had always been a business-type: a business-type in search of the right business. Raja was starting his own floor polishing business in Calcutta. It was a simple model: win a contract through a contact, rent a machine, rent the labour, and add a 15 per cent commission for yourself. Ashraf had good contacts: his uncle's younger son used to rent out machines to polish floors and offered them a ten per cent discount. They put down a fifty-rupee deposit for the machine and started their own polishing business.

Once he became a business-type, Ashraf wore freshly pressed shirts and had his shoes polished by the shoe polish boy at Sealdah Station. Ashraf earned thousands of rupees a month, which he spent on clothes, food, and his family. He never drank, rarely smoked, and never spoke roughly to anyone. He was a picture of respectability.

Ashraf's younger brother Aslam, who had accompanied him to Calcutta, was only fifteen, but he was already a goonda-type. Despite Ashraf's urging, he refused to go to school and instead worked at a local garage; he called himself a 'motor spray-painter'. It wasn't his fault, but the garage where Aslam worked was illegal. So every six months, the Municipal Corporation would send a halla gaadi full of supervisors and policemen to shut the shop, impound all the cars, and arrest all the workers for good measure. The next morning, the owner of the garage would pay a fine of thirty-five rupees a spray painter at the Lal Bazaar Police Station and the workers would be released with minimal fuss.

The problem began when Aslam started making friends in jail. Apart from an assortment of beggars, street vendors, and rickshaw pullers, the station occasionally had a few genuinely dangerous men—criminal types with police records and gang rivalries.

In jail, Aslam once met a man called Vikas Pandey who asked him for a favour. 'The police say they can release me, but I don't have any money. Can you tell my mother to come and bail me out?'

A few weeks later, Aslam was eating at a dhaba in Topsiya when Pandey walked in. He rushed up to Aslam and thanked him profusely. 'If you need anything, just let me know,' he said with a wink. From that day on, the dhaba owner refused to accept any payment from Aslam.

Ashraf told him to stop going to that dhaba.

Another time, Aslam was standing in line for a movie ticket when a man sidled up to him. 'You are Vikas Pandey's friend, aren't you? Here, take these...' and he pressed two movie tickets into Aslam's hand.

Ashraf told him to stop going to the movies.

'Aslam has fallen in with Vikas Pandey's gang of pocketmaars,' Raja warned Ashraf. 'Pandey is the ringleader of the Bihari pickpocket gang. You know what Biharis are like.'

'I'm a Bihari too,' Ashraf answered indignantly, but resolved to talk to Aslam again. But Aslam would not listen. After a while he quit his job at the garage and became a full-time goonda. Ashraf often saw him hanging around Bara Bazaar with his new friends, smoking beedis, bullying street vendors, and picking fights with other gangs. He started staying out late and would get angry whenever anyone at home asked him where he had been. After a point, he came home only twice or thrice a week—when he would sleep for the whole day and most of the night, and slip out at dawn before anyone woke up.

One morning Raja came to the house with disturbing news. Aslam had stabbed a pickpocket with an astura, a slender metal shiv.

'I didn't know he had an astura,' Ashraf exclaimed.

'Wake up, Ashraf bhai. He stole it from your old dissection kit. He slashed this man like he was cutting open a rat. Kssskh! Right across the stomach. Fortunately the man didn't die. But his friends have sworn revenge.'

'But what about Vikas Pandey? He'll protect Aslam, won't he?'

'The only thing Pandey protects is his own cock. Aslam stabbed Pandey's man. He is done for. They fought over some money—Aslam asked this pocketmaar for some money for a movie ticket, and when he refused, Aslam slashed him. Pandey is going to kill him. He is a Bihari. You should know what they are like.'

'So we went back to Patna. In two days flat we gave up the lease, and I found a small house in Patna.'

'And Aslam?'

'He came back with us. We told him to meet us at the station.'

'And the business?'

'I left the business to Raja.'

'And you never went back?'

'I did—once, but that was for some other work.'

'What work?'

'Some things a man should keep to himself. Like this. I don't have to tell you everything.'

'But it doesn't make any sense. I'm sure you could have gone back to Calcutta if you wanted. Left the matter to cool for a few months and then restarted your partnership with Raja.'

'I could, but I didn't want to. I hated Calcutta after that.'

'I can't build a proper timeline if you don't tell me things.'

'Fuck your timeline.'

6

Ashraf and I haven't really spoken since our ill-tempered argument about the timeline. We say our hellos when we meet at the chowk, but I spend most of my time talking to other people.

My interviews actually seem to be going better without Ashraf. Everyone tends to go a bit quiet when Ashraf decides to hold forth; after all, Ashraf is a 'pada-likha' aadmi, a man of learning, which obviously gives him the right to shut everyone up.

Without Ashraf, mazdoors open up to me with greater ease; they are hesitant about their past but always eager to talk about their future. Everyone at Bara Tooti has at least one good idea that they are convinced will make them unimaginably wealthy—something about the chowk breeds the wildest schemes. Its residents are invariably those who have tried their hand at practically everything before arriving at this crossing in Old Delhi. Former cooks, vegetable vendors, dhaba boys, farmers, factory workers—Bara Tooti finds a way to feed them all while they find their feet.

I once met a man in Bara Tooti who managed the bar in a rundown shack on Calangute Beach in Goa before leaving after a dispute over money. The man sitting next to him had spent many years working for a wedding caterer before he had a fight with the head cook. He told me his speciality was kulfi; the trick lay in lowering the flame to a flicker halfway through the cooking.

The most incredible scheme was told to me by Guddu, a young man of twenty-two, who ended up in Bara Tooti when his first dream ended in disappointment.

'What did you want to do?' I asked.

'I wanted to sell my kidney.'

Tired of working as newspaper boys at Lucknow Railway Station, Guddu and a friend took a train to Jaipur in search of a hospital that bought kidneys for about two lakh rupees. 'We would spend the money in full masti, and when it finished, buy a ticket to Bombay and become full-time beggars outside one of the mandirs where all the film stars come to pray.

'But the hospital said no. They said they didn't do that sort of thing any more.'

When I last met Guddu, he was planning to go back home to Lucknow and start a business with his brothers. He said he still had both his kidneys.

The theory of capital accumulation currently in fashion at Bara Tooti involves a motorcycle and two cellphones. It also requires two people to be somewhere on the periphery of Lucknow; but Lalloo is convinced it will work. 'Hundred per cent. With a system like this you just can't lose money.'

The idea is for one person to sit at a vegetable market on the outskirts of Lucknow, while his business partner roams the fields on the outskirts of the outskirts. 'The two are constantly in touch, talking to each other like on walkie-talkies. Constantly comparing the prices of vegetables in the market and in the fields. The moment the price of, say, mirchi starts rising in the market, you call up the other person and say, "Buy fifty kilos of mirchi."' The green chillies are purchased and delivered in a matter of hours on the motorcycle. At this point, the two partners exchange places, with the marketer now heading to the fields while the other monitors prices in the market. 'Do this two or three times a day, and you are set.'

'So do it, Lalloo.'

'Ah, but for that I need two cellphones and a motorcycle.'

•

Ashraf's absence has also meant that I have more time to get to know Rehaan, the young man who often hangs out with Ashraf and Lalloo and says very little. Rehaan is a bit intense, but unlike Ashraf—who has been almost monotonically gloomy for the last several weeks—Rehaan actually seems to have moods: sad, thoughtful, playful, earnest. He's also happy to respond to questions with answers, rather than see every enquirer into his personal life as a burglar who must be wrestled to the ground and beaten senseless before he makes off with a precious memento.

Rehaan comes from Sitapur, a small town in Uttar Pradesh of about 150,000 residents.

'Can you tell me something more about your town, Rehaan?'

'It has an eye hospital.'

In my early recordings, Rehaan is the humming silence in the background, occasionally breaking into the conversation in a gruff mumble, as if he were still learning how to use his freshly cracked 'man' voice. He talks of the small orchard behind his house, the land that he farmed with his elder brothers, an aunt that he sometimes sends money home with, the lack of work in Sitapur. Above all, Rehaan talks about his animals, each story beginning with a tragic loss. Along with the epidemic that once struck Rehaan's chicken coop, it appears that death cast a long shadow across the farmyard.

'We had a young lamb once, everyone loved it,' he remarks in one oft-repeated story. 'It was a really pretty lamb, but one day it died.'

'Umm...how did it die, Rehaan?''

'We had a young lamb,' he begins again. 'I think my father brought it home. I really loved that lamb. I used to give it milk to drink, from a baby bottle with a nipple. It would only drink from my hands.'

Then one day, the lamb chose to eat from the hand of another...

'One morning, I fed the lamb and tethered him to a papaya tree in our front yard. But the lamb was still hungry. He bleated pitifully; but I knew that you should never, never overfeed a young animal. So I left him there and went off.

'In my absence, someone—I still don't know who—heard the bleating and fed him some rice!'

'So?'

'He died, Aman bhai. He died! He shat himself to death. You never, ever, ever feed a young lamb boiled rice—never, ever, never.'

Rehaan also used to rear young bulbuls for bird fights; some died, some flew away. 'We used to tie a fine length of wool around their waists and tether them to short stakes a few feet apart.'

According to Rehaan, the sight of another similarly tethered bird was enough to start the fight—that and a carefully prepared diet of powdered dry fruits, raisins, and chopped papaya.

'I had one really beautiful fighting bulbul; he won every fight. Then he died.'

But today Rehaan doesn't want to reminisce about his childhood; today he wants to discuss a plan that can make him a very wealthy man—and it involves goats.

'Yes, goats—bakri. I'm telling you, Aman bhai, if you buy a goat the day a daughter is born in the house, in eighteen years you will have enough for her wedding, jewellery, clothes, and dowry. All from one goat.'

The goat in question is the long-eared Jamuna Paari goat, not to be confused with the beak-nosed Totapuri, or with the variety of mango of the same name.

On the day your daughter is born, walk down past Daryaganj to the river and buy a Jamuna Paari laila for three hundred rupees. In about eight months, around the time that your little girl is taking her first tentative steps and gurgling, your laila—now a fully grown doe—should have between two and four kids. Keep two and give the other two out on batai.

Batai—which literally means to divide or share—is when you 'lend' someone your goat in return for his feeding it. It isn't just for goats, but equally applicable for any livestock—cows, pigs, even chickens. Feeding farm animals is an expensive proposition, so by lending them out, the borrower looks after the goat in return for the milk, and the kids—when the goat births—are equally divided.

By the time your daughter is two years old, you are the master of a modest tribe of between eight and twelve goats. The does can be given out again on batai, while the rams can be fattened and sold to the butcher around Eid, when the rates are high. In time, your daughter can help out—occasionally taking the flock out to pasture, ensuring that the batai goats are well looked after, and on the joyous occasion of the wedding, at least the guests won't complain of a shortage of mutton.

'Wah, Rehaan, wah!' The goat scheme sounds perfect—a vivid illustration of the benefits of the geometric progression of goats compared to the arithmetic progressions of daughters.

Pleased by my effusive reception of his idea, Rehaan leans over conspiratorially. 'The bakri plan is great, Aman bhai, but what I really want to get into is pigs.'

'Pigs?'

'Yes, pigs. My father won't have anything to do with them, but that's where the real money is. Pigs and sugar mills.'

While the connection may not seem obvious to most, pigs and sugar cane go back a long way. Uttar Pradesh for instance, where Rehaan comes from, produces a fourth of the country's sugar and is home to about a fifth of all its pigs. Rehaan's plan involves inheriting his piece of the family land, which could take some time, and promptly shifting from their current mix of wheat and vegetables to sugar cane and then, if the family lets him, getting into the pig business.

The process of converting sugar cane juice to crystalline sugar sounds simple and profitable.

Extract juice from sugar cane and slow-cook over a low fire till thick and syrupy. Now add the trunk of the jungali bhindi plant (soaked overnight in a vat of water). The plant acts as a bleaching agent and removes any fibrous residues, and can easily be filtered out. Cook the sugar syrup some more, pour into a chakkar or mill, and occasionally sprinkle with water using a pichkari or sprinkler.

The sugar will crystallize in a few hours, leaving behind a viscous fluid called seera. Don't throw the seera; it is often fermented and used to make a local alcohol much loved by the UP jats. Don't throw the jungali bhindi residue either—it is perfect for feeding pigs.

'If you have enough residue, you don't need to feed pigs anything else.'

The concept behind pig rearing is the same as for goats—but the numbers are far greater. If Rehaan is to be believed, an adult sow gives birth to ten piglets at a time twice a year. That's twenty piglets a year! A large male pig can be sold to a butcher for up to five thousand rupees, and so within a year of spending five thousand rupees on the sow, you could earn almost one lakh rupees. And then you buy some more pigs; and then in a year, buy some more land and plant some more sugarcane and feed some more pigs—all the while making more and more alcohol from the seera. If all goes as planned, in about five years, one could own a large field, a sugar mill, a sprawling piggery, and a distillery.

'So why don't you do it, Rehaan? Let's go buy a pig today!'

'You forget, Aman bhai—my father is a devout Muslim. He'll disown me if I so much as mention a pig in his presence.'

Forbidden from chasing his dream of raising a piggery or starting a distillery, Rehaan is trying to build a future right here in Delhi. The plan is to start a business of some sort, but for that you need punji, or capital; and to raise punji in a wage market as depressed as Bara Tooti, you need to work very hard.

With his massive chest and bulging biceps that make him look a bit like a chicken that Ashraf plumped up with hot water, Rehaan works harder than anyone else at the chowk and has cut deals with several contractors to be part of their teams.

Most contractors take one look at his incredible physique and offer him work almost instantly. Rehaan isn't particularly tall, but he has serious 'mass': dense, bulky, heavy muscles that fibrillate imperceptibly when he chooses to flex them.

Back home in Sitapur, most mazdoors look like him. But no one at Bara Tooti really gets around to eating enough to sustain a body like Rehaan's. In the city, the mazdoors are much smaller, with stringy, rope-like muscles and slightly sunken chests.

'But don't look for strength in the arms, Aman bhai,' Rehaan explains. 'The back is the most important muscle. It provides a base to lift and carry. You can have giant biceps but without the back, you will not be able to pick up a newspaper.'

The key role that Rehaan plays in any contractor team is of the load bearer or palledar. For heavy loads, Rehaan says, the upward thrust has to come from the hamstrings; so your back essentially functions as a mast connecting your legs which give thrust to your arms which support the weight. With a straight back, you can channel the force from your legs right through to the weight on your arms. 'You bend your back and you could twist your spine,' says Rehaan, making a disconcerting 'snap' sound with his fingers.

Despite the strenuous work, Rehaan likes being a palledar—it gets him into a surprising number of places. Rehaan has strolled through the circular walkways of the Parliament, haunted the fire escapes of the Mantralaya building from where the chief minister of Delhi runs the city, and skulked in the landscaped lawns of the Imperial Hotel at Janpath where the rich and powerful hold conferences.

'There were white girls at the Imperial yesterday,' he announces one day. 'White girls in tiny panties and colourful bras, taking in the sun while we patched up a leak in the swimming pool.'

Distracted as I am by the image of semi-naked girls cavorting in a pool, particularly on a summer afternoon as ghastly as this one, I am more interested in Rehaan's experiences in Parliament—an edifice that many have tried to breach, but almost always without success.

After the attack of 13 December 2001, in which Parliament was stormed by armed gunmen, the Indian government spent close to a hundred million rupees on upgrading the building's security.

But two years later, a stout, middle-aged man with an unfashionably thin pencil moustache, oversized aviator frames, and a complete lack of identity papers, accomplished what five well-trained and heavily armed gunmen had failed to do. On 8 August 2003, Balbir Singh Rajput strolled into the Indian Parliament, walked about the lawns in full view of the security guards, chatted on his cellphone, and walked out untouched, unharmed, and unchallenged.

As he left, the television channel that had masterminded the prank reported that the security guards saluted him smartly and wished him a pleasant day. Rajput, a small-time actor and car driver by profession, was playing his favourite role: Shatrughan 'Shotgun' Sinha—Bollywood star of yesteryear and at that time, the Union Minister of Shipping.

On interrogation, Rajput stated that he had frequently played Sinha's double on road shows and television spoofs and agreed to impersonate him in Parliament when the television channel promised him instant fame and a subsequent meeting with the famous actor-politician. After his interrogation, police told the press that Rajput had been charged with impersonation, criminal conspiracy, and trespassing. The promised meeting with Sinha did not materialize either.

Soon after the incident, Parliament security spent an undisclosed sum on upgrading the already upgraded security infrastructure. If the Final Performance Profile released after upgradation is to be believed, Parliament is now protected by an array of devices such as 'Boom Barriers, Road Blockers, Active Bollards, Tyre Killers, Flap Barriers, Power Fences, Emergency Sound System and CCTV cameras'. Rehaan, however, pays no heed to these measures when he slips into Parliament. His daily pass suffices. On days when he doesn't feel like going to the railway station, a contractor's lorry picks him up from the footpath of Bara Tooti and deposits him deep in the heart of the Indian Parliament.

At the gate, each mazdoor is assigned a security pass and, after a stringent body search, is given a standard issue trolley and dispatched along a circuitous tour of offices, departments, waiting rooms, and meeting chambers.

Broken down to its basic components, any sarkari office—and Sansad Bhavan is no exception—works on the presumption of continuous communication between the 'officer saab', the 'clerk saab', the 'storeroom', and the 'staff'. Most offices now boast of the latest advances in telecommunication such as the telephone and intercom, yet effective administration is still premised on the twin pillars of the Ghanti and the Parchi.

According to Rehaan, every officer saab's office is equipped with the following conveniences: a television, an air conditioner, a sofa set, a double bed, two peons—better known as chaprasis—and one bell, or ghanti, to summon them. Originally wrought from the finest brass, the modern ghanti sacrifices art at the altar of efficiency and now appears as a nondescript plastic button on the officer's desk. Once pressed, the ghanti emits a crackling electronic buzz. The PA then sends across the chaprasis who are handed a note, or parchi, by the officer. In case the PA does not respond to repeated buzzing, the officer might be forced to pick up his phone and punch out his PA's extension number to draw his attention; this could constitute a serious breach of protocol.

The parchi issued by the officer usually concerns the limited functionality of some aspect of his office. Perhaps his air conditioner has packed up—exhausted by the battle of maintaining a room temperature of twenty-three degrees in a forty-five degree summer; perhaps there is a crease in his double bed. Whatever the problem may be, it is expressed in an illegible scrawl that requires the PA to leave his desk and appear in person to ascertain the exact nature of the inconvenience. Once apprised of the situation, the PA then asks the clerk in charge of the storeroom to send a replacement. The most sought-after objects in the storeroom are, in order of popularity, chairs, jugs, air conditioners, rope, tables, and the occasional almirah.

Rehaan's job consists of replacing faulty parts with the repaired units. He is not required to fix anything—for that there is a separate department of electricians, technicians, and plumbers—he is merely expected to place objects adjacent to their point of installation. Normally, in the course of an eight-hour shift, for which he is paid hundred and fifty rupees a day, there seem to be enough offices with broken furniture, malfunctioning air conditioners, and missing almirahs to keep him busy.

'One day we showed up at Sansad as usual, but instead of escorting us to the storeroom the guards took us to this other part of the complex.' There, shimmering ever so slightly in Delhi's omnipresent haze, stood a building that was never in the original layout and so should never have been built. 'It was an illegal construction, an encroachment in the middle of Parliament—hidden away where no one could see it. They told us to empty it. It's an order from the Supreme Court—no encroachment anywhere!'

'So what are they building in its place?'

'A pleasure garden,' says Rehaan without a hint of irony. 'Next we went to the old cash room and they told us to empty it out. You know what was in there?'

'Cash?'

'No, files. Mountains of files, piles of files, cupboards full of files, shelves weighed down by stacks of files wrapped in alternating bright red and dull green cloth. So many files that even the extra rooms built specially (and illegally) were filled to the brim. So many files that it finally took more than twenty trucks to cart them from Sansad to their new resting place in Lok Nayak Bhavan near Khan Market.'

'So what was in these files?'

'Everything about everything, Aman bhai. Records of every transaction ever made; of every square foot of land bought, sold or disputed; every suspect, accused, and victim; every murder, hanging, and encounter; north to south; east to west. Punjab, Sindh, Gujarat, Maratha. Sab kuch, Aman bhai—a record of everything from the number of cars in a department to the number of leaves of every Asoka tree in Lodi Gardens.'

Rehaan pauses to roll a joint; all this talking has sobered him up. I smoke silently, marvelling at how this small world in Bara Tooti intersects with a much larger universe. No one in the press wrote about the demolition of an illegally constructed room in Parliament; I'm sure none of us even knew about it. But Rehaan was there, with his hammer and his beedis, and his small pouch of marijuana tucked away in his trousers. Smoking his joint, Rehaan spent a week transporting top-secret files that reporters like me would give an arm and leg to spend five minutes with.

'Rehaan, can I come with you to Parliament one day?'

'You, Aman bhai? Why?'

'Just to see what palledari work is like.'

'I can't take you into Parliament, Aman bhai. The security is really strict. Plus, you don't really have the body of a palledar.'

That much, I concede, is true. As consolation, Rehaan offers to take me to a place that he promises me is as exciting as Parliament.

•

'Attention, all passengers. Passengers please note that Train Number 5708 Amrapalli Express from Amritsar to Katihar will be arriving shortly on Platform Number 3.' It is 3:40 pm at Old Delhi Railway Station; I am here on the directions of Rehaan and have been instructed to look out for his supervisor: a short, bald, and portly man called Babulal.

On first impression, I have to admit that Old Delhi Railway Station is scarcely as exciting as the Indian Parliament. On a scale of ten, I'd give it about two and a half for excitement, and only because the man standing next to me is arguing with a railway employee about the best way to transport a batch of live chickens. 'Just wait till the train comes in, Aman Bhai,' Rehaan says and slips away as he doesn't want to be seen with a pesky journalist.

At a distance, I can make out Babulal striding along Platform 3; he looks like an unlikely candidate for the post of the overlord of Old Delhi station. But like the truly accomplished, Babulal has risen to his position of prominence on the backs of those who have consistently underestimated him. He has never made the mistake of appearing either brilliant or ambitious; but, in his defence, his job has never required him to be.

Babulal is the head foreman of one of Old Delhi Station's bigger contractors—someone called 'Anand sir'—and is responsible for moving more than a hundred tonnes of cargo a day. His job requires him to be steady, dependable, and relentless, and my sources at Bara Tooti insist that he possesses all three qualities in abundance.

I walk up to him and introduce myself, but it is apparent that Babulal has absolutely no interest in either befriending me, or telling me about his life, work, or interests. Babulal, it appears, is a man of few interests.

Rehaan has described railway work as perfectly attuned to the rhythms of the marketplace. The job is to load and unload goods trains as they roll through Old Delhi Railway Station.

Workers can either work on a semi-permanent basis where they are paid three thousand five hundred rupees a month for a four-day week, or can choose to work on a dehadi basis for two hundred and fifty a day. Those working on contract are free to pick up dehadi elsewhere on their free days.

As a professional journalist, I obviously cannot take anything Rehaan has told me for granted without corroboration from an independent source, and who better than Babulal? Precisely what sort of work is railway work? Is it a form of azadi or gulaami? Dehadi or permanent? Is Babulal a thekedar? Or does he work for one? Maybe he is some sort of subcontractor: a chotta thekedar. An abundance of questions, but given Babulal's reticence, and the imminent arrival of the Amrapalli Express, I'm struggling to make some sort of headway when the announcement lady starts up again: 'Attention, all passengers...' Already delayed by almost an hour, the Amritsar–Katiyar Amrapalli Express is due in the next fifteen minutes.

Eager to bring the train back on schedule, the announcement lady with the mechanical voice has decreed that the train will stop for only twenty minutes instead of the customary thirty.

'Come along,' Babulal says and hurries off down the platform. I switch on the recorder and give chase.

He first walks up to the PCO booth under the staircase and hands over a crisp five-hundred-rupee note. 'Give me the most tattered ten-rupee notes you can find.'

He then strolls further along the platform to the slender steel girder from which hang several steel locks. 'Harrison Seven Levers, Harrison Seven Levers,' he mutters as he shoves his hands into the cavernous pockets of his cotton trousers and retrieves several crudely wrought keys, each capable of unlocking several different locks produced by the same manufacturer. He takes his time choosing the right lock, comparing shank lengths and the strength of the locking mechanism, and once satisfied, walks to the head of the platform where the train is expected to stop.

As a man with a press card, I cannot be wished away, but I have been instructed to stand at a safe distance and well out of the way. The Amrapalli Express rumbles in at 1605 hours. The lady with the mechanical voice announces the arrival of the train, and Babulal's team pounces upon it. I skulk behind a bunker of wooden crates, recorder in one hand, notebook and pen in the other.

16:06 hours: Babulal leaps aboard even as the driver grinds the train to a halt. He wrenches open the lock with one of his many skeleton keys and throws his weight against the sliding door.

16:08 hours: Babulal is still struggling with the door. It seems to be blocked by boxes jammed against it from the inside. Seven mazdoors are wrestling with the handle, practically wrenching the door off its rails. I can see Rehaan hovering around at the back of the team, bouncing on his toes like a pro athlete about to take to the field.

16:10 hours: The door is finally open. Chotta, a slender, wiry member of the team, had slipped through the tiny child-sized space between the door and its frame and moved the box pressed against the door channel. The door slides open all at once even as Chotta shouts out a warning. A four hundred kilogram crate bursts out of the train car and flies in my direction, bouncing off the platform with a dull thud followed by the sharp crackle of splintering wood. Fortunately I am some distance away.

16:15 hours: Eleven more gunny-covered wooden crates have been flung out onto the platform and arranged in a neat grid. The team is running on schedule. Babulal is slowly returning to ground state; the vein on his forehead gradually subsides, the hand holding the beedi has stopped trembling. He pulls out a large pink delivery challan from his pocket and laboriously notes down the names and addresses scribbled across the crates in black permanent marker. The team scurries back down the platform and returns with a handcart piled high with identical gunny-wrapped crates with different markings. Loading begins.

16:17: hours: The train is scheduled to leave in the next eight minutes. Loading progresses smoothly and on schedule. Floor space in the bogie contracts and expands rhythmically as the boxes are arranged in horizontal terraces that start from the corners and work their way inwards like an ascending staircase which requires that every successive box be raised only one level at a time. Babulal has finished filling out his delivery challan, and is already planning for the next delivery.

16:20: hours: Panic! A large hairy man in a migraine pattern shirt rushes towards the bogie. He is shouting at the top of his voice. He is waving his hands excitedly. He is threatening to bugger Babulal and the entire team. He is Pramod, the head contractor Anand sir's eldest son.

16:21 hours: Pandemonium. Of the twelve unloaded crates, six—marked 'SNC' in green permanent marker—were meant for the onward journey. They should never have been unloaded. Babulal waves the delivery slip at Pramod, as if to indicate that this was not conveyed in the paperwork—but there is no time for arguments. The train will leave in four minutes.

I can see why Rehaan is such an asset to the team. Everyone else relies on a combination of skill and physics to manoeuvre the boxes into place, daintily flipping hundred kilogram crates using their shoulders as fulcrums and their hips as pivots. Rehaan, meanwhile, is simply muscling his way through the carriage, lifting up boxes and flinging them aside with insouciance.

16:22 hours: With three minutes to go, things are unravelling for Babulal's team despite Rehaan's heroics. Sensing the delay, the engine driver sidles up to Babulal. 'The train shall leave immediately, Babulalji. It would be terrible if some of your cargo is left behind.' Babulal reaches into his pocket for the bundle of tattered notes and hands the driver a handful.

16:23 hours: Perched in their eyrie-like offices above the platforms, the high officials of the Indian Railways peer out at the chaos unfolding on Platform 3. The engine driver's visit has not gone unnoticed. Package Babu ruffles his feathers, Signals Babu stretches out his wings, TT Babu smiles wickedly and one by one they prepare to wing down silently to Platform 3 where the Amrapalli Express lies beached with her engines heaving and her innards spilling out onto the platform.

16:25 hours: 'This train was scheduled to leave two minutes ago, Babulal. TT Babu will be very upset if it gets any later.' Package Babu smiles even as he attempts to keep a straight face.

'Sahib, it shall leave immediately. Just give me two minutes.'

'But immediately is not in two minutes, Babulal. Immediately is right now.'

'Sahib, you tell me what I should do.'

Package Babu raises himself onto the balls of his feet and rocks back onto his heels; he continues this giddy motion even as he looks down at the pointy toes of his shoes. They are scuffed. Package Babu is not happy. Northern Railways has tasked him with ensuring that the train leaves the station on time, which it won't. He also wants shiny-tipped shoes, which his aren't. 'I need new shoes,' he remarks.

'And TT Babu?'

'I will handle TT Babu. His shoes are fine.'

Babulal reaches into his pocket for more tattered notes; their raggedness is his silent protest.

16:29 hours: The train is now officially late. Fortunately there is only one more crate to go. If they can make it by the twenty-fifth minute, they might be able to stave off TT Babu; he only comes down past the seven-minute mark. Package Babu's walkie-talkie crackles. TT Babu is getting impatient.

'Tell Babulal the price is rising.'

'Don't worry, TT sir. The train is leaving immediately. The train shall leave in one minute.'

'Immediately is not in one minute. Immediately is right now.'

16:30 hours: The bolt slides home with a bang. Babulal fits on his lock; his colleague at Katihar will have a skeleton key of his own. The faulty delivery has meant that the team has moved eight tonnes in twenty-five minutes. Package Babu barks out a command into his walkie-talkie. The engine driver blows his whistle. Signals Babu changes the lights from red to green. The Amrapalli Express pulls out of Old Delhi Railway Station, rolling smoothly on wheels greased by Babulal and his team.

The team loads the six crates onto their modified wheelbarrows and wheels them off down the platform towards the godown. Rehaan waves to me as the mazdoors leave the platform. There is no hurry now; the Amrapalli is the last train of the day shift.

•

I can't help but feel worried for Rehaan—not that he needs my concern. He seems too young, too full of hope to survive a place like Bara Tooti. I keep thinking of telling him to go home to his family, his goats, and his fighting bulbuls, but Rehaan seems to be enjoying the thrill of living in a city like Delhi and the occasional visit to the swimming pool of the Imperial Hotel.

'Rehaan is a good boy, but he has it all wrong. There are easier ways to make money than to spend one's time in the company of farm animals or working like a mule. Raising punji is the easy part. A man has to have a business-type brain.' Ashraf and I are talking again, on the condition that certain topics are off-limits. 'Look at Kalyani, she makes money night and day—even as she sleeps, money finds its way into her pockets. And look at us. This is what happens if you stay too long in Delhi.

'When you first come here, there is a lot of hope, abhilasha. You think anything is possible. You have heard all the stories of people who have made it big in the city. Slowly, as time goes by, you start wondering what you are doing. One year, two years, three years, and you are still on the footpath. But people say, have faith, bharosa—something will happen. But slowly you realize, nothing will happen, and you can live the next five years just like the last three years, and everything will be the same. Wake up, work, eat, drink, sleep, and tomorrow it's the same thing again.

'So you start fantasizing about returning. You think of the lush green fields, the cool, pure water, the healthy food. You suddenly decide that you were wrong all along; there is money to be made in the village, especially for a man with your experience. But one morning you wake up to realize that living isn't so much about success as it is about compromise—samjhauta. A samjhauta with life, where you stop wanting to be anything at all. After enough time in Delhi, you even stop dreaming—you could go crazy if you think about it too much.

'This is a brutal city, Aman bhai. This is a city that eats you raw—kaccha chaba jati hai. For you, all this is research: a boy tries to sell his kidney, you write it down in your notebook. A man goes crazy somewhere between Delhi and Bombay, you store it in your recorder. But for other people, this is life. There are pimps lurking at every corner, waiting to spirit you away if you so much as talk to them. Behind Jama Masjid, there used to be an organ market—anyone could go and offer to sell anything. I've heard of people selling their eyes, kidneys, bits of their liver—practically anything. Once they get into Delhi, people see the roads, the crowds, the cars, the madness; people lose their balance in this city.

'At Koria Pull near the railway station, young sixteen-, seventeen-, eighteen-year-old boys are sold like cattle to be worked on fields in Punjab. Do you know that?

The boys will walk out of the train with nothing—just a bundle of clothes and a few beedis. A man will walk up to them, give them food and a place to sleep, and next morning he will say, "There is this theka in Noida, just get onto the truck." You get onto the truck and that's it—khatam! You wake up in Punjab and a sardarji puts you to work in his fields and that's where you stay for the rest of your life.'

'Doesn't anyone run away?'

'Lots of people try; but they have no money. No one in Punjab gives you any money—you get food and clothes and that's it. Finally, how much can you run, Aman bhai?'

7

It takes a chat with Lalloo to make sense of Ashraf's moody outburst. Two drinks down Ashraf can coldly describe the two of them as 'medium-type friends', but the truth is that Lalloo is Ashraf's only friend in Delhi. Ashraf is articulate, witty, and occasionally brilliant; but after three days of drinking, it is Lalloo who finds ten rupees for him to buy tea, take a shit, and get back to work. It is Lalloo who pulls Ashraf back from confrontations with the police, arguments with Kaka, and fights with other mazdoors at the chowk.

Ashraf maintains that he is a peaceful drunk, but that is largely due to Lalloo's calming influence. Ashraf had introduced Lalloo to the safedi line and for that alone Lalloo will stand by Ashraf—till the day one of them vanished.

'Because people vanish all the time, Aman bhai. One day they get onto a train or jump into the back of a truck and you never see them again; you never know what happened to them. Maybe they got lucky and became rich; maybe they went to jail and are still there; maybe they had an accident and died. But no one looks for them, because no one really misses them any more. It's been ten years since Ashraf spoke to his mother, Aman bhai; he's terrified there will be no one to look for him when he's gone.'

As I find out, people didn't just lose themselves in transit; in Delhi, people are picked up off the street in broad daylight, incarcerated for years, and never seen or heard of ever again. The man behind many of these disappearances turns out to be a thickset man in his early forties: stocky, greying, fit for his age, clad in the nondescript brown favoured by government employees, unremarkable save for a pair of shiny white Campus sneakers.

Sharmaji is a senior officer at the Beggars Court at Sewa Kutir, in Kingsway Camp in North Delhi. His job is to catch beggars and have them tried and punished in court. Begging in the national capital is a serious offence, and under the Bombay Prevention of Begging Act, 1959, the Department of Welfare can arrest all those 'having no visible means of subsistence and wandering about, or remaining in a public place in a condition or manner, [that made] it likely that the person doing so exists by soliciting or receiving alms'. It isn't just the alleged beggar; the law also has provisions for sending the family and dependants of the accused off to a remand home if the court feels they might turn to begging.

None of the men I know at Bara Tooti have any visible means of sustenance. If I saw Ashraf lying drunk on a pavement one evening, I wouldn't know what to make of him. So how can Sharmaji tell a beggar from a working man who is merely poor?

'You can tell by looking at the hands. The rickshaw pullers, for example, have rough calluses here.' Sharmaji grabs my hand and points to the arc where the fingers join my palm. 'It's the rickshaw's hard plastic handles. The skin first blisters, then the blisters become calluses and the calluses form little ridges.'

'They also have big, bulging calves,' Sharmaji adds as an afterthought. 'And some of them sit funny.

'Mazdoor hands are different from beggar hands. They have calluses too—but their nails are scuffed from handling bricks and sand. You won't see a rickshaw puller with scuffed hands. Safediwallahs tendy to be tall and lanky and are usually sprinkled with paint dust. Carpenters are Muslims and usually carry tools. Never, Aman sir, never trust a man who travels without his tools.'

Sharmaji, raiding officer for the Department of Social Welfare and the source of these ethnographic insights, has rather soft hands himself—the sort that might be subjected to the occasional massage of Pond's Cold Cream. But he has strong fingers and well-rounded shoulders: the anatomy of a man used to grabbing people and shaking them about.

'Beggars don't have any calluses. How can they if they never work? Also, a working man—no matter how poor he is—will always look you in the eye when he talks to you. But beggars? No, they can't look me in the eye.'

'Now take you, for instance.' He shakes my hand vigorously, somehow managing to point at me with my own fingers. 'No one will mistake you for a beggar even if you dress up as one.'

I try and imagine if I would look Sharmaji in the eye. He reminds me of a particularly feared mathematics teacher from school—a man who appeared reasonable at most times, but could be moved to violence by completely innocuous acts. My teacher too had a habit of grabbing students by the shoulder and jerking them about, an experience I found intensely disorienting.

This should be a period of frenetic activity for Sharmaji and his team; the minister heading his department has promised to make Delhi 'beggar free' in time for the Commonwealth Games in 2010. Sharmaji's department has deadlines to meet, beggars to deport, and cases to file. The target for the year is at least five thousand beggars. But the reception area is empty, save for the two of us, as are the small courtrooms.

Sharmaji's raid vehicle has broken down, making it impossible for him to drive around the city chasing beggars. The wheels of the Delhi government do not move any faster for its own departments and so Sharmaji has been told that a new vehicle will arrive 'in some time'.

'Right now, the only beggars we have are those rounded up by the Delhi Police. But they don't know how to read hands. The police can't tell a beggar from a beldaar.'

Suddenly I am very afraid for my friends.

'The police don't even know how to catch them.' Sharmaji is disconsolate. 'There is a special technique. You can't just stop anywhere and run at them. Now where would you go to catch a beggar?'

'I don't know. A traffic light?'

'Wrong!' he says with some satisfaction. 'Correct but wrong. Don't worry, it is a logical mistake to make. You may *find* them at a traffic light, but you cannot *catch* them at a traffic light. You see the difference?' He grabs my wrist again.

'We all know that beggars stand at traffic lights, but if you try and catch them, they often run off straight into traffic. The result? Accidents, traffic jams, and the public also gets upset.'

Instead Sharmaji and his team stake out at the major temples in the city. 'It is the fault of our culture. If people spend lakhs of rupees in feeding the beggars, why would anyone work? All they do is sit and wait to be fed. This is not how you give discipline to the nation.'

At temples, the beggars tend to be more docile and less likely to escape through rush hour traffic. 'Temples, train stations, bus stands. Here you will not only find beggars, but also be able to arrest them.

'It is best to arrive after they have been fed. Mid-afternoon to late evening, when they are drowsy and there aren't too many pilgrims around.'

Unsurprisingly, Sharmaji also has a photographic memory. 'I never forget faces—never. I will never forget your face. It is stored in my brain's computer.' Since the Begging Act prescribes 'Not less than one year and not exceeding three years for first time offenders. Ten years for repeat offenders,' raiding officers like Sharmaji are often asked to testify if they had ever arrested the person before. 'Obviously nobody gives the same name twice. So we have registers and registers of the same people—only stored under different names and addresses.'

Most departments would have buckled under the weight of such voluminous and apparently useless data, but not the Department of Social Welfare which has already begun to computerize its registers. Equipped with the latest advances in biometric technology, the Beggar Information System or BIS 2.1 is 'like our own passport office'. The machine is designed to store the details of every single person arrested by Sharmaji's team: name, date of birth, place of birth, photograph, and biometric fingerprint. Once registered, the information is stored 'forever', implying that recidivists will no longer fool the judge by claiming that they got off a train in Delhi, were robbed of all their possessions, and were begging to get enough money to go back home. Once arrested, the beggars will be marched off to the registration room, photographed, fingerprinted, and presented before the court. If convicted, they are taken to one of twelve prisons set aside for beggars and locked up for a minimum of one year and a maximum of three.

'So can I see this system?' I am eager to witness the information revolution at work. 'Where is the machine stored?'

'On the first floor.' Sharmaji is unsure. 'It isn't really working these days. We have called the technician, but after a point he stopped taking our calls.' Occasionally, the receptionist—who is on his lunch break—calls the technician from a different phone number from another department, but the technician has wised up to these tricks. 'He says some part is missing and he shall come only when it arrives from the warehouse.'

'I just want to see it. We don't need to use it or anything.'

'Come along then.'

Sharmaji turns the key, and there it is, under a shroud of white plastic dust covers: the Beggar Information System Version 2.1. It is a record of every beggar with the misfortune of crossing Sharmaji and his team. The machine is a rather bland-looking personal computer with little to distinguish it apart from a rather clunky-looking webcam and what appears to be a small plastic matchbox.

'Is this it?' I find it hard to conceal my disappointment.

'Well, yes. To be honest, we were a little surprised ourselves. We expected something a lot bigger.'

'So this is the biometric reader?' I pick up the box and toss it in my hands casually.

'Careful, Aman sir, careful. This is not a toy, this is a biometric device. The beggars place their thumbprint on the glass and the webcam takes their photo. That way we have full identification.'

'So is the database searchable?'

'There are a few small problems,' Sharmaji says sheepishly as he fires up the machine. The designers had failed to read the tender document carefully. The tender, freely available on the internet, clearly asks for 'an interface to identify the habitual beggars at the time of reception by scanning the thumb impression or keying in other relevant information to establish the identity', but this crucial detail had slipped the designers' mind. Instead, the firm (whose name Sharmaji coyly refused to reveal: 'You are from the press, no? He he he') had provided two separate interfaces—one for data entry and one for data search, thereby doubling the time required for registration instead of halving it. It was this particular software error that the technician appeared unable to fix till the 'missing part' arrived.

The other, more pressing problem lies with the scanner itself. Though the tender had mandated a 'scratch-resistant' scanning surface, the scanner—as befitting any high-tech gadget—was extraordinarily sensitive to dust. It worked best when recording images of clean, slightly moist thumbs that, when pressed down onto the glass surface, flattened ever so slightly to allow for a true record of the fingerprint in question. 'But these beggars,' the exasperation in Sharmaji's voice is palpable, 'their hands are so dirty, so filthy, that the scanner just cannot pick up the image.' All they got were blurry smudges that the machine was unable to identify, let alone catalogue and search. 'So we started washing their hands before registering them. But that took too long.' The department also tried bathing them—but, after a bath, the beggars look 'just like anyone else'. How then can the judge make his decision?

'Now we register once manually before the hearings. And then again on computer in the evenings. That way we have complete records.'

'But you can't search them.'

'We can.' Sharmaji is quick to defend BIS 2.1. 'It just takes some time, that's all. In India, all everyone wants to do is criticize.'

As I get up to leave, Sharmaji points out three freshly bathed men leaving the reception centre. 'The judge gave them a second chance.'

I catch up with one of them on my way out. 'Are you a beggar?'

'Of course not, I'm a snake charmer.'

'So where's your snake?'

'Sharmaji asked me the same question. The Wildlife Department took it away.'

•

Unlike the Beggars Court, which has an office with a signboard, the kidney snatchers of Ashraf's nightmares turned out to be harder to find. I tried hanging around Koria Pull, waiting for someone to approach me, but kept bumping into drug dealers who followed me at a safe distance and whispered, 'Hashish?' every time I turned around.

A year after Ashraf and I had our conversation about the kidney racket in Old Delhi, I found myself at a police press conference in Gurgaon. On a tip-off from a young police officer from Moradabad, Manjul Saini, the Gurgaon Police had stumbled upon a racket in which a team of rogue doctors had illegally transplanted more than six hundred kidneys in the last nine years.

At the time of the conference, the lynchpin, Dr Amit Kumar, was still at large. It would be another few months before he would be arrested in Kathmandu.

The modus operandi was scarily similar to what Ashraf had described: pimps prowled the labour chowks in and around Delhi and lured them away with the promise of work. Thereafter, the labourers were forced to undergo operations in which the doctors robbed them of their kidneys, gave them a nominal sum of money, and threw them back on the street. The kidneys were then sold to wealthy Indian and foreign buyers.

When the police raided one of the clinics run by the group, they found two labourers who were just about to be wheeled into the operation theatre. For three other labourers though, the police arrived too late.

Soon after the press conference, I went across to the Civil Hospital in Gurgaon where Nasir, Salim, and Shakeel were recuperating after their forced surgeries. I asked them if they remembered anything from their ordeal.

They remembered a great deal.

●

The room zoomed, and slipped and slid and panned; the walls closed in and in—so close, still moving, can't stop them, the room zoomed and slid and panned. The ceiling fan turned one way and then another. Everything seemed like something else and then the same thing happened the other way around.

A pain—a jagging pain, a deep scar, a long cut, a careful tear, a knife mark. Down his side he felt the criss-cross of surgical thread. He felt the sheet rub against his back. He felt the pillow under his head, he felt his bladder pressing up against the curve of his stomach. Nausea dribbling through his body, he felt last night's meal pressed up against his chest, crawling up his throat—a spider, a big hairy spider with spiky razor-tipped legs. Dal chawal; it was dal chawal—yellow dal with pyaaz ka tadka, cooked by the skinny man who looked Bihari. It had taken a day or two for the routine to be hammered out. It is hard to portion out responsibilities when two Nepalis with guns threaten you every time you open your mouth.

The tall Muslim with the red beard had disappeared soon after he offered the job. It was to be a big one, in Ballabgarh, at least five to six months: one hundred and fifty rupees a day, plus free food and accommodation. They were getting labour from all across the country. They needed a few experienced hands, which is why they had come down to Choona Mandi Chowk for a safediwallah. They would provide all the paints and brushes.

He said yes. The Muslim's accomplice put him onto a Roadways bus. They got off at India Gate and into a waiting car. The driver of the black Maruti Esteem told him to sit low on his seat. The car ride lasted almost four hours. He fell asleep several times. They gave him an injection, took some blood. They told him it was a rush job for a government agency; they needed to take blood tests for the health scheme.

'Health scheme?'

Yes, health scheme. Didn't he know the government now offered free health care to all labourers?

Even dehadi ka labour like him?

Even dehadi ka labour like him. After all, this was the sarkar of the aam aadmi. Everyone has got to be on the health scheme.

Once they stopped the car and took out a large box from the back. They put a drop of his blood into what looked like a painter's palette. They told him not to worry; he had passed the blood test. Now he would certainly get the job.

It was dark by the time the car reached the eerie abandoned house in what looked like a jungle. By now he was really tired; they practically carried him in. That's when he saw the armed Nepali guards watching over ten cowering mazdoors.

They stayed in that house for almost a week. There were provisions of rice, wheat, dal, and a cooking stove to prepare their meals. No paints or brushes though. Inmates disappeared every other day and more arrived to take their places, but the guards neither answered his questions nor let him address them to anyone else, and so he never found out where the older inmates went and where the new ones had come from. They all looked like they had been picked up from chowks across Delhi, but were probably from all over the country.

One night they woke him up at one o'clock and told him to get dressed. They told him to lie down on the back seat of a car and keep his head down. They drove for about ten minutes before they stopped and changed cars. This time he was put into a black Hyundai Santro and told to lie down once more. They stopped outside a large black gate. The guard got out and knocked three times. The gate opened, and they pushed him in at gunpoint and strapped him into a stretcher.

A man in a green surgical mask and gown walked up to him and slid a needle into his vein. He felt his muscles spasm and the ceiling swirled into a fast spinning vortex before he passed out.

He awoke on his side, vomiting violently, bringing up nothing but fluid. A nurse, her face obscured by a surgical mask, handed him a tissue to clean himself. 'What have they done to me, Nurse? What have they done?' She stared back impassively; she had 'Chinese eyes'. He grabbed her hand and pleaded with her to tell him, and so she did.

He lay back in his stretcher and ran his hand along the long gash, mouthing gentle consoling sounds. 'You're going to be okay,' he said. 'You're going to be okay.'

•

My phone rings; it is 1 am.

It's Ashraf.

Satish is sick.

If Ashraf is to be believed, Satish is dying. Satish is coughing up blood, Satish is going deaf, Satish can't talk, Satish can't walk, Satish can't work. All Satish can do is sit in a corner with a rag to his mouth, holding in the blood that leaks out of his lungs and onto the pavement in scattered flecks that look like paan stains but aren't.

Who is Satish?

Satish is a young boy, like Rehaan. He is very shy, but he is very smart. I haven't met him, because he usually works at Choona Mandi, a chowk in Paharganj not far from Bara

Tooti, but Ashraf loves him like a younger brother. Satish taught Ashraf how to varnish wood, Satish taught Lalloo how to win at cards. Satish is the only person Rehaan listens to. But Satish is dying. Well, right now he is sleeping, but he is very sick. I must come tomorrow as early as I can.

I will come tomorrow. Goodnight, Ashraf.

Goodnight.

three

LAWARIS,
or Forsaken

1

The old man adjusts the bandage on his head, looks about, and beams widely at all present.

To his left, a middle-aged man uses a large cotton swab to staunch the blood that gushes from a large hole in his throat, even as he tries to soothe his hysterical wife. On his right, male nurses strip a plump eighty-year-old down to his underwear, rub his arms, feet, and chest with conductive gel, and stick him with electrodes. Somewhere down the hall, an elderly lady suddenly keels over and goes into a faint. 'This, Doctor, this! This is what we were talking about,' a swarm of relatives babble, relieved that the old lady has shown her symptoms in so unmistakable a fashion.

'Move back! Give her air. A nurse will handle this. Nurse! Monitor vital signs.'

The middle-aged doctor nervously scratches the bald patch on his head. Scribbling down a rash of prescriptions, he moves to the next bed, to the eighty-year-old now sprouting electrodes.

'Symptoms?'

'Sharp pain in the chest, sweating, breathlessness. Possible cardiac arrest.'

The doctor scans the readings, stares closely at the man's face. He reaches out, checks his pulse, examines his pupils, and asks the patient to say a few words. A few nervous scratches, and he is ready with a diagnosis.

'Acute indigestion! Stomach pump, and overnight observation.' A few hurried assurances later, the doctor is ready to move on.

'A round of dressing for patient on Bed 2—recurrent post-operative bleeding... Bed 4, oxygen. Bed 12, saline drip. Bed 7? What is he doing here? Refer to Orthopaedics!' Onward ploughs the doctor, wading through a sea of fevers, concussions, and sunstrokes till he finally arrives at the old man with the bandage on his head.

'Yes?'

'Doctor, for the past few days I have been troubled by incessant itching all over the body. I cannot rest, I cannot sleep, my mind is in turmoil. Doctor, I must be admitted at once.'

'Don't worry, Uncleji, it is a normal part of the ageing process. Nurse, possible senile atrophy of the skin.'

'No, no, Doctor, this is not normal. I have been old for many years now. I must be admitted at once.'

'Don't worry, Uncleji, skin conditions do not require hospitalization. I will prescribe an appropriate cream for your skin, and a sedative to help you feel better. Do you have any other trouble?'

The old man thinks for a moment. 'I have no sensation in my legs,' he proclaims. 'Fainting fits, dizziness, nausea, splitting headaches... I must be admitted at once.'

'Sir, I understand you are unwell, but we have an admission policy.'

'No, Doctor, *you* do not understand. I cannot go home!'

The harried doctor and a now nervous old man stare at each other, each aware of the silence that has settled over the emergency room. The masked ward boys take a welcome moment of rest before wheeling out the next stretcher; the nurse looks up from her patient on Bed Number 4 and critically examines her shiny red nails through her translucent latex gloves. Prone patients raise themselves up on their elbows to watch the unfolding drama, unsure of who deserves their sympathy: the doctor strapped with limited resources, or the old man cast out from his home.

'We have a shortage of beds in the general category, Uncleji.' The doctor seems to have made his decision. 'I am transferring you to the Neurology Department. Maybe they will have some space.' He scribbles a referral on the old man's pink slip and calls for a stretcher.

Satish and I sit quietly as we wait our turn. Satish is dying, even as I sit by him. He is a young, slender boy— in his early twenties—with a hollowed-out chest and a wispy moustache caked with blood. The nurse has placed us right at the back, far away from the other patients. She knows what it is; I know what it is. We just need a doctor to write it down on paper.

•

Down the road from Azad Market, up past the morgue at Baraf Khana, a wave of peaks and troughs ascend from North Delhi's market districts up to the more rarefied realms of Delhi University. Cycle rickshaws stop at the base of the hill, defeated by the steep first section of the ascent. Passengers are directed to the line of autorickshaws that, for a fee of five rupees per person, ferry patients and visitors up the hill to the small tea stall outside Bara Hindu Rao Hospital, Malkaganj.

Auto drivers wait till they have at least six passengers packed into their vehicle designed for three, and only then do they begin the slow trek up the hill—an agonizing journey played out in the company of complete strangers. The strangers, in themselves, are not a cause of concern: Delhi is a city of chance encounters spawned by the failure of public transport.

Along the city's extensive roadways, strangers hang out of the open doors of the same public bus, holding onto each other like lovers, reaching out for reassurance whenever the bus hits a bump; harried commuters come together to hire autorickshaws that charge per trip rather than per person; a gaggle of sleep-deprived passengers exchange notes over cups of tea as they discuss the repercussions of delays at the railway station.

But the ten-minute journey to Bara Hindu Rao has none of the intimacy witnessed when groups of people are crushed together and forced to 'adjust'. Here, passengers stare straight ahead, refusing to make eye contact with each other, unwilling to converse with anyone apart from the driver. Conversations might go beyond discussing the rising price of dal to more uncomfortable places: places where the man with a raw open wound covered with a somewhat clean cloth discovers he is sitting next to the lady with a fungal skin infection, and the boy burning with fever leans against the man who might have leprosy.

The driver plays his part in enforcing the no-talking rule; the person breathing down the back of his neck could be a pukka tuberculosis case. He leans forward on his seat and guns the throttle. The engine howls like a whipped dog.

•

'Phoot Path, Bara Tuti, near Garg Sweet House,' the conscientious receptionist writes with a slow and heavy hand. All patients must register before they see a doctor; all fields on the registration card must be filled. An address must be found—even when there isn't one. 'Lawaris,' he adds for good measure. 'Casualty Ward—through the door and take a left.'

The senior doctor on duty sits deep inside the Casualty Ward, his desk screened off by green curtains. Various other doctors sit adjacent to him along an L-shaped table, conducting spot examinations on patients and assigning them to different departments.

Today, the ward is populated by a large number of policemen accompanied by forlorn-looking 'suspects'. Bara Hindu Rao is the accredited hospital at which all suspects arrested in the northwest zone must get their formal medical examination before an appearance in court.

'What happened?' asks the doctor, noting the bruises on the young man's body.

'I fell down. Hard,' says the suspected chain snatcher with the red hair. 'The road was slippery.'

'But you have bruises, not grazes.'

'Some people in my cell were drunk. They attacked me. Only the intervention of the police saved my life.'

The doctor nods thoughtfully, but makes a note in his record: 'bruises; suspected muscle contusion due to heavy compressive force w. blunt object.' It is unlikely that the court shall notice his observations, but he is duty-bound to make them; he is a good doctor.

Another suspect lies on the bed next to the doctor's table. His eyelids flutter gently as a constable attempts to revive him. He is a slight, mousy man with a dejected face; he went into a swoon when they brought out the syringe for the blood test.

'Probably has a fear of needles,' remarks the ward boy.

'He is here because he ran away with a girl he loved and her parents reported it as a kidnapping,' says the constable. 'He says she loves him too, but let's see what she says in court.'

'Turn your back to me, and now breathe deeply.' It's Satish's turn to be examined by the doctor. The doctor prods Satish's stomach suspiciously. 'You smoke, don't you?' Satish shuffles nervously, unsure if he is still eligible for treatment if he smokes. 'Do you get the shits?'

'Yes, yes.' Now on surer ground, Satish nods vigorously.

'Medical Emergency Room, second floor. Warden, send the next patient in.'

Most patients approach Bara Hindu Rao only when a mild fever, ache, or pain has been ignored to the point of exacerbation—so even when their illness is far from life threatening, the patients arrive convinced that their condition qualifies as an emergency. Upon entry, they are surprised to learn of the existence of not just one, but at least four different emergency wards—Medical, Neurological, Orthopaedic, and Paediatric. What then to do with a hyperactive child who has broken her arm? With an ageing aunt prone to spontaneous fainting fits? With a mazdoor who has a seemingly incurable cough and fever?

The Casualty Ward is designed to eliminate such confusions—which is why it is on the ground floor adjacent to the reception (the signs say 'Reception cum Casualty'), while the emergency rooms are tucked away in the building's far corners: Medical Emergency is on the second floor, adjacent to the Paediatric Emergency; Orthopaedics is on the first floor, near the X-ray room. The receptionist sometimes forgets exactly where the Neuro Emergency is, but the ward boy then reminds him that is another wing altogether.

The Casualty Ward functions like a sorting station in the warehouse of illnesses that is Bara Hindu Rao Hospital. After a perfunctory examination by the senior doctor, patients are dispatched to one of several different departments scattered across three floors in two separate buildings. The urgent cases are dispatched to the emergency wards, the rest are directed to OPDs.

'Third door on the right; bald man sitting behind the smallest desk; toilets are on the first floor; skin specialist is not available on Thursdays; the doctor is in; the doctor is out; the doctor will be right back.' Sharmaji is the gatekeeper to the doctors' chambers, a position he has held for the last eighteen years. His job is to regulate the flow of patients into the Examination Room. A skinny, perpetually tense man, he speaks in the short staccato bursts of a professional giver of directions.

On most days, each doctor is sent two patients at a time so that, having finished with one, he can instantly turn his attention to the other. On crowded days, Sharmaji sends patients in batches of three so that two sit in front of the doctor, while the third stands to one side—waiting for a free chair. Of course, each patient is accompanied by at least one 'next of kin', and so the Examination Room, at any given point, has between ten and twenty people jostling for space.

Sharmaji breaks for lunch at two o'clock when the registration counter opens once more. Afternoon registration lasts for exactly one hour and is reserved for what Sharmaji calls 'hard diseases': heart trouble, arthritis, rheumatism, and other chronic conditions. In the thirty minutes of his lunch break, Bara Hindu Rao Hospital reconfigures itself into an entirely different hospital.

As a multi-speciality health services provider, it is several hospitals at once: each room doubles up as a different department depending on the time of day. In the time that Sharmaji takes for lunch, Room 201 transforms from General OPD to Chronic OPD; the adjacent room 202 switches from Diabetes to Nephrology, with a Respiratory Diseases doctor coming in three days a week. The OPD is shut on Sundays, except on the second Sunday of every month—when it functions as a free health camp for senior citizens. On other floors, entire departments are often clubbed together in associations that offer an insight into the mind of the sarkar: the Department of Dermatology also functions as the Department for Sexually Transmitted Diseases with a special focus on VD, and the Department of Gynaecology doubles up as the Department of Family Welfare and Child Health which distils itself into the Department of Family Planning. The only rooms that never change position are the Casualty Ward and the emergency rooms—they are the fixed poles around which the hospital orbits.

The last door at the end of a long dark corridor, the Medical Emergency, where we now find ourselves, is a cramped but well-lit room with large, grimy grille windows that look out over the Delhi Ridge.

When they aren't taking rounds of the ten-odd beds, doctors sit on a tiny table pushed against a window in the front, cramped into immobility by another large desk that is piled high with bandages, cotton wool, and IV bottles, and talk through a connecting aperture to the nurses who have a large comfortable room of their own. Conversation is usually brief as the glass pane of the connecting aperture is rendered opaque by the plaster strips that cover the pane's surface, with the result that the doctor is unsure who he is speaking to. On the left side are large square patches that are probably used to cover messy gaping wounds like those of the man on Bed 2; the right side of the frame has longer, rectangular pieces meant for securing IV needles, and on the bottom edge are long, thin strips used for taping up gaps in dressing. One broad strip of plaster runs along the length of one of the panes—its function appears to be to hold the pane together. It isn't easy to manipulated a roll of plaster when wearing latex gloves, so a ward boy has been tasked with ensuring a regular supply of sticking plaster in its various shapes.

'Show me your slip.' Having dispensed with the last two patients in record time, the doctor has turned his attention to Satish's admission card. 'Hmm, you smoke, do you?' Satish's head oscillates in a non-committal fashion. Undeterred, the doctor directs his next question to me, 'Attendant, how long has he had these symptoms?'

We may be friends, lovers, family, or acquaintances; but on entering a sarkari hospital, a couple is immediately divided into 'mareez' and 'attendant'. The hospital is committed to assisting the mareez; but a shortage of nurses, assistants, and ward boys implies that every mareez should ideally be accompanied by an 'attendant' who may get a day pass made at the gate and provide doctors with a vivid description of the illness—a description that the mareez may or may not be in a position to provide.

'At least a month; we came here because today he started coughing blood.'

'Blood? Chest X-ray, first floor. Don't look at the patient directly in the face. Please keep your mouth covered at all times.'

●

'One second, Bhai saab, ladka ya ladki?'

The X-ray has been taken, it will take about forty-five minutes to develop. Satish is lying on a stretcher somewhere in the large hall. My reverie is interrupted by a middle-aged woman carrying a large basket.

'What?'

'Ladka ya ladki? Boy or girl?' She repeats in English. She rummages through her basket and holds up a set of tiny overshirts. 'One hundred per cent cotton. All different colours. Cheap prices.'

'I don't have a baby,' I mumble.

'Oh, then don't wait outside the maternity ward.'

2

Held up to the light, the darkened plastic sheet reveals a latent image of the criss-cross lattice of bleached white bone wrapped in a milky haze of flesh and muscle. In the centre of the frame lie the two large dark sails of Satish's lungs bisected by the clearly etched mast of his spinal cord. At the bottom, just slightly off the centre, his heart shows up as a burst of bright light oozing into the dark shadows of his lungs. 'The cardiac silhouette is enlarged,' muses the doctor. 'But that could just be a problem with the X-ray.'

The worry is the creeping lesions that appear as localized conflagrations on the dark green X-ray. The doctor asks for Satish's card once more and scrawls out a diagnosis.

'This is a referral slip,' he explains, 'for RBTB Hospital at Kingsway Camp. Go there right away.'

It's a ten-minute drive from Bara Hindu Rao to RBTB but the auto drivers always ask for too much. En route to Bara Hindu Rao, a patient might still retain a degree of privacy regarding his ailment, but when I ask an autorickshaw to take us to RBTB the driver doesn't need to look at Satish's X-ray to know what's wrong.

'RBTB case?' he asks. 'Eighty rupees.'

Originally called 'Silver Jubilee TB Hospital', the Rajan Babu Tuberculosis Hospital was set up in 1935 to commemorate the twenty-fifth anniversary of the coronation of King George V, and renamed after Independence. Spread out over seventy-eight acres of green, leafy land near Delhi University's North Campus, RBTB is the largest tuberculosis treatment centre in Asia with over a thousand beds housed in four-storey wards, but a surfeit of patients means that admission is far from easy.

A panel of masked doctors sit behind a long table, occasionally nodding the next patient in. The patient is seated on a wooden bench approximately six feet away from the table and instructed to place a handkerchief in front of his face and to look away while coughing.

The masks are not necessary as long as the patient does not cough directly in one's face, but, at this stage, patients are still unfamiliar with the mannerisms of their disease. They are still caught by surprise when a cough suddenly wells up, still unnerved by the sight of blood. If admitted, they will, in time, unlearn the habit of looking at people while talking to them, of making eye contact while listening. After a few weeks, the hand shall instinctively rise to cover the mouth even as the diaphragm convulses for that distinctive gritty cough that brings up mucus, spittle, and blood. At present, patients are still capable of that occasional careless sneeze that could cover the entire panel with a cloud of deadly germs.

'And what will you do then, huh?' says the gruff attendant to the sneezing patient. 'Who will cure you if you infect the entire department?' The attendant is unmasked—the doctors have told him that the size of the TB bacillus is smaller than the pores of the mask filter.

'Next!'

Though committed to providing free treatment to TB patients, RBTB Hospital is a tertiary hospital; it is meant for those who have already tried to treat the disease at primary and secondary care centres and failed. Centres at every stage provide the patient with a referral slip that offers entry to the next tier; and so patients who approach RBTB directly are directed to a care centre on a lower tier.

The first five minutes of every interview at RBTB are consumed by a review of the evidence: the patient and the family must prove that they have exhausted all other means of medical redress before they appear before the panel; without a referral slip, it is impossible for the doctors to even interview the patients—it's against the rules. Prescriptions, X-rays, referral letters, and test results must be marshalled in a convincing manner before the doctors come to their decision. Most patients are too ill to move unattended; they sit back on the bench as a family member coaxes, pleads, and harangues the doctors into admitting their relation.

The doctors rarely ask any questions. As one doctor later told me, 'The problem is that everyone who comes to RBTB has already been told to say that they regularly cough up blood in their sputum...' and a lot of them do. They sit silently, inscrutable in their masks, wincing to themselves as relatives and patients talk of how far they have come and the difficulties they have overcome in their quest to reach RBTB. With the hospital running at full capacity, every patient admitted means another booted from his or her bed and declared fit to go home.

Patients are allowed about ten minutes to plead their case. The lucky ones are put onto stretchers and bundled off into one of the hospital's many wards; the rest are asked to return when their condition worsens.

'But, Doctor saab, we have travelled two hours by bus to get here; we cannot take him back...'

The doctor shakes his head with sincere regret.

'Next.'

In the waiting room, I'm picking up pointers on how to convince the doctors. Everyone present has a theory. The crowd is undecided on the profile of a likely 'admit case'. The fifty-five-year-old carpenter from Tilak Nagar is of the opinion that doctors prefer younger, 'softer' cases. 'It makes sense to treat those who have a good chance of recovery and a whole life ahead of them. What's the point of wasting medicines on someone who might die in the next few years anyway? You have a good chance: the old must make way for the young.'

But the thirty-year-old seamstress from Dilshad Gardens thinks that the doctors prefer 'urgent cases', 'because the others can come another time when there are more beds'.

'The doctors prefer poor patients because if the sarkar doesn't take care of the poor, then who will?'

'No, they prefer rich cases, because all the doctors are actually looking for bribes.'

'You should come with your family because those with relatives get priority. The hospital doesn't have enough staff to look after everyone.'

'If you come with too many people, the doctors will send you home because they will assume you will be well looked after.'

'If one of you can cry, it might help your case.'

'Only with a male doctor; with a female doctor it could be tricky. If her husband doesn't listen when she cries, why should she listen when you cry?'

'Next!'

'Number 35!'

'Wake up, Satish, that's you!' I give him a shake and half carry him in. We take our seats on a long wooden bench facing the long table of four masked doctors.

The first question is directed at me.

'Are you a social worker?'

'No sir, I am a journalist.'

'Are you writing a story on this man?'

'No sir. I am trying to help him.'

'The press is always criticizing. Never any helpful suggestions. Just point fingers.'

The panel speaks as one mind, the masks making it difficult to pinpoint the source of any one remark.

'The press does not determine the facts. The press does not consider the limitations.'

'Yes sir.'

A pause. The masks seem disappointed; I have surrendered so easily.

'How do you know this man?'

The attendant outside has warned me of this question. 'Do not say you know him. If you do, you will have to stay with him in the hospital. Say you found him lying on the road, and they will put him in the lawaris category and assign him someone from the ward.'

'Sir, I saw him lying on the road.'

'And you brought him?'

'Yes sir.'

'Journalism is the wrong profession for you. You should be a social worker. Does he have a referral letter?'

'Yes sir, and an X-ray from Bara Hindu Rao.'

'Fill out this form. Patient admitted. Next!'

To
The Medical Superintendent
Rajan Babu Tuberculosis Hospital

Dear Sir,

This is to state that I, Satish Kumar, s/o Lallan Singh, am a pavement dweller and lawaris case (without kin). Due to my illness, I am without work and am poor, destitute, and helpless. It is requested that my meals be provided free of cost for the duration of treatment at this hospital.

Sincerely,
Signed

Signature/Imprint of Right Thumb of the Patient

A doctor dictates the letter, I write it out, and we force Satish's thumbprint on it. 'We will take it from here,' says the ward boy, and Satish is carried off on a stretcher.

3

'See, see. Right here.'

'A bullet wound?'

'No, no.' Bhagwan Das tries to shake his head but is constricted by his shirt which he has pulled up over his head to give me a better view of his large and completely hairless stomach. We are discussing the genesis of the neat, circular scar just above his right hip.

'The pipe, the pipe.'

'What pipe, Bhagwan Das?'

'Arre, the plastic pipe I pissed from! After the accident, the doctors put in a pipe and I pissed out of my hip for the next three years. When the minivan ran me over, my bladder burst like a water balloon. So they had to give me a pipe to pee from.'

'So then?'

'For three years, I walked around with the pipe and a bottle. For three years I couldn't piss.'

'And now?'

'Now I can piss—it's all God's grace. That's when I decided to stop driving an autorickshaw and picked up my father's old tools. The pipe is gone now. I piss... I piss normally now. But the scar is there. Three years without pissing, can you imagine?'

Honestly, I can't imagine. I believe him when he says it was horrible, I don't need to see the scar. But this is RBTB Hospital—all everyone does is trade stories about illness and accidents; and each story is presented, picture book-like, with accompanying scars or stitches.

We are sitting in a dingy staff room on the third floor of one of the male wards. Bhagwan Das is in the midst of telling me why he came to RBTB.

Bhagwan Das is a man who, of his own volition, spends more time with the patients than anyone else in the hospital. He isn't the ward boy who ferries patients between wards and clinics, he isn't the nurse who makes them take their medicines, he isn't the doctor who checks on them every now and then: he is the barber who wipes flecks of dried blood from their lips, lathers their cheeks, and spends the day shaving them, his face a few inches from their mouths. Their mouths!

There are no gaping wounds at RBTB, no shattered bodies covered in bloodied bandages—at RBTB Hospital it's the mouth. The mouth is the festering sore, the suppurating lesion, the source of contagion.

But Bhagwan Das has no fear of the disease; he has survived the foul air of RBTB for more than seven years without once succumbing to the common cold. Not a cough, not a hint of a fever, not a day missed due to illness. He looks patients in the face when he addresses them; he doesn't cringe when he touches them; his grip is as steady as his razor is sure.

He sauntered into Satish's ward one afternoon, just as I was leaving, and shouted out what I subsequently learnt was his trademark greeting. 'Main hoon Bhagwan Das nayi, aaj kis kis ne nahin banayi?'

He came up with the greeting a few years ago, 'I am Bhagwan Das, the barber, who hasn't shaved today?' Of course, it sounds better in Hindi, it has a ring to it. The patients like it. It cheers them up, gives them something to look forward to. Without that, a TB hospital can be a pretty depressing place.

It's a strange place to set up shop. It's one thing to be assigned to a TB ward; it's another to choose to come there of your own accord.

Bhagwan Das comes from a line of barbers. His father ran 'Punjab Hairdressers', a successful salon in Shahdara. 'But I never wanted to be a barber,' he says. 'Instead I became an auto driver.' And then he had the accident with the minivan.

'After the accident, it was a year before I could walk again. A man can do a lot of thinking in that time.'

When I hear stories that involve a patient lying flat on his back for six months I often wonder how the patient ever emerged from the episode with his mind intact. It happened to a friend of mine who dislocated his hip in a motorcycle accident and spent three months in a hospital; but then he was in love and spent his time writing letters to his girlfriend who eventually married him, so I suppose it all ended well.

For Bhagwan Das, the first two months, when his body still possessed a memory of mobility, were the worst. But in three months he had transformed into another creature;

the soles of his feet no longer missed the unyielding texture of floor and the skin on his back—initially prone to rashes and bedsores brought on by his prone posture—adapted to the task of bearing his weight.

The pain changed pitch as well: from a white hot agony radiating outwards from his shattered hip to a dull, gnawing, and persistent ache that moved along his spine, spread outwards along his ribcage, and then upwards to his shoulder blades.

But would he ever walk again?

In the first month, the doctors were non-committal at best. 'You should walk again, but then you never know about these things.' On other days they adopted a more cheery, and paradoxically more depressing, demeanour. 'I am sure you will walk again. Never underestimate the miraculous healing powers of the human body.' They also told him to be happy: 'Happy people heal faster.'

They were more optimistic in the second month, and by the third, had assured him that he would almost certainly walk again. As the terror of paralysis receded, he found his thoughts turning to the future. He knew he would never drive an autorickshaw again, but the only other thing he had ever done was help out at his father's barbershop in Shahdara.

And then he met Ram Babu. When he stepped out of hospital a year later, Bhagwan Das often wondered if Ram Babu had existed at all, or if he was a figment of his sedative-influenced imagination. The nurses and doctors had changed since he was admitted, and so did not know of the man who had occupied the bed adjacent to Bhagwan Das's for just one week. Das remembers little of that time except that he and Ram Babu had long, profound discussions on the meaning of this life and the path of the virtuous man.

He just had to close his eyes to recall Ram Babu's serene bearded face, with those twinkling playful eyes. 'I was once admitted in RBTB Hospital,' Ram Babu would say. 'There you will find patients suffering. Why not devote yourself to easing their pain?'

'But the patients at RBTB need a doctor; I am just a barber-turned-auto driver,' Bhagwan Das would reply.

'They suffer not from their illness, but from their abandonment. You wonder how a mere barber can ease suffering? Do you have the courage to shave the needy? Do you have the strength to give them company, maybe for just five minutes as you shave them? To make them feel like someone cares and isn't scared off by their illness?' It was on Ram Babu's directions that he changed his name from Bhagwan Singh to Bhagwan Das, literally, servant of god.

'Did you ever meet Ram Babu again, Bhagwan Das?' I asked.

'No, never. I never found out who he was, or what he did. But our conversations in the hospital stay with me to this day.'

On 17 November 2001, Bhagwan Das picked up his old shaving kit and scissors and stepped into RBTB Hospital with a prayer on his lips and a handkerchief tied tightly about his face. The first day at work was terrifying; he had never seen such ill people before. But every time he wavered, he thought of Ram Babu's beatific face and resolved to continue at RBTB.

Initially, he spent the mornings working at the hospital and the evenings at his father's shop in Shahdara. But once word spread that he was shaving patients in a TB hospital, his evening practice dwindled to a few regulars, who insisted on bringing their own scissors, towels, and razors. After a few unsuccessful attempts at reviving his evening business, Bhagwan Das embraced the path shown to him by Ram Babu and threw in his lot with the patients at RBTB.

Twelve wards, at least thirty patients per ward, between eighty and a hundred paying customers a day, approximately ten rupees per customer, and no competition for their business. No rents, no bribes, no overheads, no staff salaries. A risk of illness and possibly death—but certainly safer than driving an autorickshaw.

'One must accept that living is itself a risky business,' explains Bhagwan Das. 'To live is to risk death. Some risks, like the risk of an accident, are shared equally; other risks, like TB, can be minimized.'

Pulmonary tuberculosis, as an intern once explained to Bhagwan Das, is spread primarily through airborne germs exhaled by those afflicted by the disease. Once in the lungs, the infection results in scarring of the lung tissue leading to shortness of breath and wracking blood-laced coughs. In a hospital scenario, or even elsewhere, it is impossible to avoid these germs altogether; the only solution is to boost the body's natural defences to ensure that the bacilli are swiftly eliminated when they enter the body.

Bhagwan Das wakes up at six o'clock each morning and follows a routine that has the rigidity of a ritual. Three rotis with vegetables, curd, and a quarter chakki of butter. Then he dons his work clothes: one of three identical pairs of plain white shirts and trousers that are washed every day in a solution of Dettol and detergent. At work, he is careful to avoid any contact with blood or saliva, and at the end of his shift he washes his hands with two separate soaps—an antiseptic one and a neem one—kept especially for this purpose. The dirty clothes are stuffed into a plastic bag and dropped into their antiseptic solution on returning home.

'I am very disciplined. No meat, no alcohol, no paan, no gutka, and no beedis.' Except on Tuesdays when, like all barbers, he takes his weekly holiday and sits out in his small veranda in his house in Shahdara, and pours himself a stiff whisky and lights a cigarette. 'A quarter bottle of whisky and three cigarettes—that's all I allow myself.

'On Tuesdays I think about how so many people lose everything and die in a hospital—sad, sick, and lonely. It's important to think about these things: Where are you going? Where are you coming from? What could happen if this happens? What will happen then? I am healthy now. My wife loves me; my son is working in a call centre. But I could fall ill tomorrow. What if my wife deserts me? What if my children disown me?'

'What will you do then, Bhagwan Das?'

'I'll lie down on one of these beds, safe in the knowledge that the ward boys will look after me and the doctors will heal me.'

'But who will shave the barber?'

'That is a good question. Who will shave the barber?'

•

I'm travelling in Aligarh when my phone rings.

'Mister Sethi?'

'Yes.'

'I am calling from RBTB Hospital. Please speak to Mr Satish.'

Satish is not doing well at all and has demanded to speak to me. A doctor has agreed to make the call; unfortunately, it is of little use. I bellow down the phone, but get surprisingly little response.

'Yes, you are right,' the doctor admits, having taken back the phone. 'He is quite deaf.'

'So how am I supposed to speak to him?'

'Well, I thought he could at least speak to you! Don't worry, it's just an allergic reaction to streptomycin. He will be fine.'

'Well, he doesn't sound fine.' In the background I can hear Satish mumbling incoherently.

'Everything is under control. Please come as soon as you can.'

I make a hurried phone call to my sister. She agrees to go down to the hospital with a friend of hers. She calls back triumphant.

'It's fine. We've fixed everything. He just needed a change of underwear. They hadn't bathed him since he was admitted a month ago.' They bought a fresh set of clothes, two sets of underwear, a mug, a bucket, and some soap. She said he seemed much happier.

4

Satish Kumar, Bed Number 53, Rajan Babu Tuberculosis Hospital, is dead.

He was discharged on 11 July. They said his TB was in recession, they said he would make it. But then he got worse. Finally, a social worker from the Sewa Ashram took him away to spend his last days in peace. He died on 13 July 2006 at Sewa Ashram, Narela. A nurse at the Ashram told me that the last rites were performed at the electric crematorium at Rajghat.

No one at the mandi even knew when it happened. They still don't know. I have found out today. I am preparing myself to tell them.

I found out when I went to the hospital and saw someone else in his bed. Singh Sahib, right across in Bed 56, told me that the bed had been reassigned to another patient. He told me that several people had been discharged in the same week. Singh Sahib is an emaciated shell—TB has hollowed him out. Satish is only one of the many he has seen die around him. He has been in Ward M 13 for almost four months without dying or being discharged—a record of sorts. He spends most of his time lying flat on his back, alternately calling up his 'Chandigarh walle sardarji', who doesn't pick up his calls, and castigating his family via telephone for not visiting him. It used to be a running joke in the ward that no one who walked in with a cellphone could walk out without having dialled a number for Singh Sahib. But now there is no one left to laugh any more.

Everyone has gone: Manoj the electrician in the yellow shorts who used to fill Satish's water bottles; Krishna the aspiring social worker who used to run down to the STD to make calls for Satish; Pratap Singh, Satish's self-appointed caretaker, and former colleague at Choona Mandi; and even Ammi and her son Salil. Ammi, who used to stay up nights nursing Satish's cough with glucose solution.

Towards the end, I knew Satish would not make it. They kept giving him his medicines, but he wasn't getting any better. By the second month in RBTB, he had lost so much weight that his body lost its sense of proportion. His eyes bulged out from his shrunken face and cheeks, his jaw jutted out awkwardly. His head seemed abnormally large for his emaciated body and his hands looked too heavy for his twig-like wrists.

An allergic reaction to streptomycin had worsened his condition, rendering him almost entirely deaf; antibiotics-induced jaundice had turned his nails, eyes, and skin yellow. The doctors assured me his hearing would return once he was taken off the drug, but that won't happen now.

Despite Ashraf's repeated promises to see Satish, he didn't visit him once. Every time I visited the chowk, he would ask after Satish and reveal another facet of their unusual relationship. 'Satish was actually Lalloo's friend,' he said. 'But the three of us became very close. He worked in Choona Mandi but we spent most evenings together.'

But he never went to see Satish; never dropped in in the evening; never took the gang from Bara Tooti along to cheer Satish up. 'Hospitals depress me,' he offered when I confronted him. 'We are all waiting for him to come back.'

After a point, Singh Sahib says, Satish just lost his will to live. Three months in hospital had worn him down. Then a young boy across the room died and someone else took his place. Then Pratap Singh was discharged and went home to his village. Then Krishna, then Ammi and Salil, and finally Manoj. Only Satish and Singh Sahib remained—staring blankly at each other across the narrow aisle. And then the social workers took Satish away. Singh Sahib tells me about the Ashram; I call them, which is when they tell me of Satish's death.

Now there is only Singh Sahib in Bed 56. Someone else has taken Satish's place—the same way he took someone else's. Satish's earthen water pot is gone from the bedside table, as is his spare underwear that used to hang on the headrest. His pink plastic bowl and steel tumbler have been replaced by plastic Pepsi bottles (now filled with water), a loaf of Harvest Gold bread, and a solitary boiled egg. The hospital authorities claim to change linen as often as possible, but the sheets still bear unwashable traces of their many previous occupants. A man-sized sweat stain darkens the length of the bedsheet—a trailing after-image of countless coughing, sweating, retching bodies.

During what were to be his last days, Satish often vacillated between going home and staying back in the hospital. Some days he declared he wanted to leave for his hometown Bina by the next train. 'It's one of Madhya Pradesh's bigger junctions, Bina Junction—everyone knows of it.' He had a phone number: a simple six-digit number with a bulky, imposing area code. He last dialled it ten years ago; he wondered if the number would be the same—so much had happened since he left home at thirteen.

Ashraf often wondered why Satish left home. What sin could have forced him out of the cosy sleepiness of Bina into the uncontrolled chaos of Delhi? What could he have done at thirteen? Theft? Murder? Rape?

Satish spoke little of his motivations, but Ashraf spent hours agonizing about the past of the quiet painter. 'He must have stolen some money from his father's pocket, that could be the only thing,' Ashraf concluded. 'But how much could it have been? Now he will go home, and I will give him five hundred rupees and even if his father doesn't forgive him outright, his mother will; and she will make his father forgive him!'

But Ashraf never did convince Satish to go home. Satish listened quietly to Ashraf's remonstrations—smiling grimly, and occasionally shaking his head in disagreement.

Satish once borrowed my cellphone and dialled a number from memory: 07580 221083. The phone rang for a while, and then stopped—so the number still existed. Fortunately Bina was a small town, its phones insulated from the incessant violence of changing numbers and differing exchanges. He dialled the number again, and handed me the phone. This time someone answered the phone.

'Hello, who is this?'

'I'm calling from Delhi. I want to speak to Lallan Singh of Paliwal.'

'Sorry, you have the wrong number. There is no Lallan Singh here.'

'Wait, wait, is this Bina, Madhya Pradesh? I am calling from Delhi.'

'Yes it is, but...'

'Lallan Singh is your neighbour. He doesn't have a phone. Please call him, I am his son's friend speaking.'

'No, I'm sorry, Lallan Singh's not my neighbour. You have the wrong number.'

'No, wait, one last question. I'm calling all the way from Delhi. Is this the kirane ki dukaan near the doodhwalla?'

'No, it isn't. I'm sorry.'

Bina is a small town, and the numbers don't change. But people do. People change and people move—from one house to another, from one mohalla to the next. Boxes are packed, trunks are brought out from under the beds, telephone numbers surrendered, security deposits collected, and the numbers, just like hospital beds, are transferred to other homes and families. They are circulated among new sets of relatives, new colleagues at work, new sons in different towns, new daughters now married and settled. But the old numbers are never forgotten; they lie in a tiny pocket diary carried in the inside pocket of a shirt worn in Bara Tooti. A phone number in a small town near a big railway station—waiting to be dialled once more, ten years too late.

'Hello, I'm calling from Delhi, can I speak to Lallan Singh?'

'I'm sorry, but this isn't his number any more.'

•

My phone rings.

It's Ashraf.

He has heard about Satish.

He's crying.

I had gone straight to Bara Tooti once I left the hospital, but Ashraf wasn't there. Kaka told me he had gone looking for work with Lalloo. Kaka gave me a cup of tea. 'For free,' he said, 'in memory of Satish. He was a good boy, a nice boy, a quiet boy. Always paid on time. He was a polite boy—never did danga, never did gaali-galoch, never drank and got into fights.'

Ashraf found good work that day. He bought mangoes. 'Maybe I'll take some to Satish,' he told Kaka. 'I'll sit with him for a while and give him a mango.'

Then Kaka told him; so he's called me.

He wants to go away from Delhi, far, far away. When will I come next to Bara Tooti?

I will come tomorrow. Goodnight, Ashraf.

Goodnight.

•

'Electric crematorium at Rajghat? Not bad, Satish, not bad at all.' Ashraf forces out a smile between drags of his beedi. 'Rajiv Gandhi was cremated there, wasn't he? He must have gone straight up to heaven.'

'These things are important.' Ashraf is slipping into one of his monologues. 'If you are cremated in the wrong place, who knows where you might end up. I was personally present when Dr Hussain was buried. I bathed the body. There was no one else. Who would wash him and dress him? We called a qazi; he said, "Ashraf, you were like his son. You do it." So I did it.'

'How is Lalloo? I haven't seen him in a long time.'

'Lalloo is upset. He is drinking somewhere. You know what Satish did to Lalloo, don't you?'

'No.'

'Satish was a young boy, but he drank like a bastard. At the time, Lalloo never drank. He had a small stand at Choona Mandi where he sold parathas and sabzi for five rupees a plate. Satish was the one who got him started on drink. One time they sat down and drank for two days straight, non-stop. They ran out of money, so they drank on credit at one shop in Choona Mandi itself. Then they ran out of credit there, so they came to the corner shop at Bara Tooti. Then they ran out of credit there, so they moved to Kalyani's and drank there. By the time Kalyani threw them out of her house on the morning of the third day, they were in debt for about a thousand rupees, maybe more. But when they got back to Choona Mandi, Lalloo's stand was gone! Everything. The plates, the spoons, utensils, kerosene burner, even the stale atta and sabzi—all gone. That's when Lalloo went a little crazy, and he's been like that ever since.'

'You never mentioned this before. You told me Lalloo lost his shop at cards.'

'Yes, yes. He and Satish and this other man were playing cards together. And then they started drinking. Anyway, it doesn't matter now, does it?'

'Why were they still friends? Didn't Lalloo hate him after that?'

'It wasn't all Satish's fault. He didn't force Lalloo to drink; there must have been some reason why Lalloo drank like that. Kuch toh majboori hogi/yun aadmi bewafa nahin hota/raat ka intezaar kaun kare/din mein kya kya nahin hota.'

This was one of Ashraf's favourite sayings, 'There must have been compulsions/For a man to go astray/Why wait for nightfall/When anything can happen in the day.'

If Lalloo really was selling parathas in Old Delhi when he could have been living with his estranged wife and wealthy father-in-law in Gorakhpur, I can imagine him suddenly cracking one day, but why was Satish drinking like that?

'He was young. People do stupid things when they are young. Satish also played a lot of cards. And I think he sold his kidney.'

'What?'

'I think so. That boy was capable of anything—even selling his own kidneys. He must have done it for the money. The problem with Satish was that things always worked out for him somehow, so he kept doing stupider and stupider things. Then of course, he got TB.

'Even now, look at what's happened: Ram Avatar died last week; the police took his body to the Baraf Khana and will probably donate it to science. Satish dies; he goes to the electric crematorium in Rajghat where Rajiv Gandhi was cremated. So Ram Avatar's spirit wanders from one medical school to another where college kids tear out his organs and put them into jars. Satish goes straight to heaven.'

5

'Aman bhai, you need to send Ashraf away,' Lalloo shouts into my ear. 'Since Satish died, something has broken inside him.'

'Where do you want me to send him?' I yell back over the noise of my motorcycle. 'We can't just push him onto a train.'

'Why don't you ask him? I've tried, but he told me to mind my own business.'

'What about Patna?' I slam the brakes and up-shift frantically as a scooter nips out of a side lane. I'm not quick enough on the clutch; the engine gargles and stalls.

'Oho, sorry, sorry,' Lalloo apologetically wipes away the white powder he has spilt all over my back. 'I don't think he will agree to go to Patna.'

We are headed to Kasaipura, a ten-minute ride away from Bara Tooti. I spotted Lalloo at a paint store in Sadar Bazaar and offered him a ride. Ashraf is already there, paring the wall down to its base coat. Lalloo is taking along the ingredients for the patti—a paste of porbander mitti and paint that they shall slather onto the naked wall and leave to dry overnight.

As I struggle to kick-start the motorbike, Lalloo explains the purpose behind the various powders stuck to my sweater. 'The patti works like a binder between the wall and the paint; without it the paint has nothing to hold on to. Tomorrow, we'll arrive early to smoothen the wall with emery paper and then slap on the paint.'

'What colour does the maalik want?'

'Pink.'

'Why pink?'

'Wait till you see Kasaipura.'

The smell of blood is overwhelming; it prowls along the alleyways of Kasaipura like the ghosts of the buffaloes that lie dismembered before me. The floor is sticky—a chip-chip texture that holds my shoe soles just a fraction more than the tarmac road outside, but could as easily turn slick and treacherous. It's a bit like walking on congealed blood—in fact, that's exactly what it is.

Lalloo walks alongside, pushing me out of the way as a young boy pulls a wagon loaded with buffalo heads through the narrow passage. Just behind him, a wagon of hooves, a wagon of haunches, a wagon of ribs—and Mohammed Ashraf.

'What are you doing here, Aman bhai?'

'Lalloo brought me.'

'Lalloo's a chootiya. Come, I was stepping out for a beedi anyway.'

'What's the problem? I just want to see the place.'

'There is no problem, but you don't always need to go everywhere and see everything.'

'True, but...'

'This is a butcher's area. It's sensitive, Aman bhai. People get nervous when you presswallahs walk in with your recorders and cameras and ask all these questions. Now let's go!'

He calms down once we are outside. 'People are worried that you will write about how you saw a thousand heads of cattle in a cart. All you need to do is mistake a dead buffalo for a dead cow and tomorrow a mob will burn the place down.' He looks like he's upped his drinking again. I realize, not for the first time, that a significant number of my conversations with Ashraf are when he's either slightly maudlin or hungover. It could explain why my timeline is still incomplete.

Ashraf shivers and hugs himself; he's obviously working his way out of a week-long binge. 'It's a horrible time in Delhi,' he offers by way of explanation. 'It's the todh-phodh. The demolition.'

•

'Mr Kutty? Is Mr Kutty present?' The judge looked up from his desk, the lawyer appearing on behalf of the Municipal Corporation nodded his assent.

'Mr Kutty, Additional Commissioner, Engineering, Municipal Corporation of Delhi, is present in court today,' continued the judge. 'He has placed on record the details asked for by us. According to him in 2001 there were 2,765 cases of unauthorized construction; in 2002 there were 4,385 cases of unauthorized construction; in 2003 there were 3,749 cases of unauthorized construction; in 2004 there were 4,466 cases of unauthorized construction; and in 2005 there were 2,934 cases of unauthorized construction, making a total of 18,299.

'We find that there has been a steep rise in unauthorized construction each year... What does it show? It shows that the officers of the Municipal Corporation of Delhi, its engineers, are hand in glove with those who indulge in unauthorized constructions and that without their active or passive connivance it was not possible for such mushrooming of unauthorized constructions in the capital of this country.

'We make it clear that in terms and on the basis of the said report unauthorized construction in the area should be demolished forthwith by the MCD at the expense of the owner/occupier of the property concerned. Status report of the Committee appointed by this Court be filed within a period of two weeks.'

The gavel falls with a bang—and two weeks later, the city is aflame.

•

Looking back now, it's hard to map out everything that happened after the 14 December 2005 Delhi High Court order that called for the demolition of all unauthorized constructions in Delhi. The todh-phodh, as the regulars at Bara Tooti called it, spread rapidly across the city as the Municipal Corporation's demolition teams fanned out into markets and residential colonies. Some colonies, like Seelampur in the east, went up in flames as rioting traders and workers flung stones at policemen and the police responded by opening fire. A fourteen-year-old schoolboy was shot through the throat as he made his way home from school. The newspapers bemoaned the disruptions to traffic. The Delhi Police offered its security cameras to spot illegal construction in real time. The Minister of Science and Technology contemplated the use of GIS mapping to keep a close watch on the fast mutating city.

In January of 2006, the todh-phodh appeared in Sadar Bazaar as a creeping silence that made its way up the radial roads from Connaught Place. First the markets closest to the railway station shuttered their shops; further west, safediwallahs in Choona Mandi near Ramakrishna Ashram dropped their brushes and picked up their bottles and went on a prolonged drinking binge. Fearful of the circling bulldozers, Kalyani declared her place off-limits till further notice and went back to her main business of sifting grains. In Bara Tooti, Kaka contemplated doing the same—his shop was of dubious legality as well. An uncle had promised to help him out in case the police came, but had then stupidly aligned himself with Madanlal Khurana, a former Delhi Chief Minister who now had neither a party nor a support base. 'If only Tauji had stayed with the Congress,' Kaka would say with every cup of tea he poured, 'my children wouldn't have to worry about my health. I am an old man, Aman bhai, I can't keeping taking stress like this.'

For Ashraf and Lalloo and Rehaan and everyone else who sat around at Bara Tooti, the todh-phodh meant that no one in Sadar wanted any work done at all. Not very many labourers in Bara Tooti built a house from the foundation up; large projects like those were usually given out to contractors who brought their own mazdoors, supervisors, and foremen. At Bara Tooti, Ashraf and Lalloo converted balconies into bedrooms, divided a large living space into two bedrooms using partitions, or made subtle encroachments onto the pavement by extending the front of the house to the footpath.

After the todh-phodh began, no one was willing to risk additions to their already overburdened homes. No one even wanted any paintwork done, fearing that a bright new coat would draw attention to the architectural peculiarities of their home. For the two months, mazdoors lived off their meagre savings, assuming that the demolition drive, like most sarkari drives, would slowly run out of steam and stop. But as the drive continued, many left for home. Others, like Ashraf and Lalloo, walked the bylanes of the bazaar in search of work. The only work to be found was where there was a wedding in the family, or in places like Kasaipura.

'Kasaipura is one of the oldest parts of this area.' A chai and beedi have loosened Ashraf up. He waves away the offer of a milk rusk, but bites into a fen. 'It is run by a very powerful clan—the Qureshis. Good connections with all the political parties. The butcher wanted pink—he said the blood doesn't show up so much on pink. I suggested red, but he said, "Isn't there enough red around you already?"'

I see the butcher's point.

'And pink is a good shade for summer,' says Ashraf, displaying his delicate sense of aesthetics, 'light pink and light green. But with these light colours matching is very important.'

'So Ashraf, where do you want to go?'

'Nowhere. Patna ka toh no chance. All my friends have become collectors and policemen and lawyers and judges. What face shall I show them? I can't be a mazdoor in my own town, Aman bhai.'

'So who builds the houses in Patna?'

'Runaways from Kanpur.'

•

The todh-phodh dragged on all through the summer; mazdoors at Bara Tooti grew more desperate. On one of those oppressive afternoons, Kaka confided that he had saved enough money to buy his son an aerated drinks stall in East Delhi and so was thinking of shutting shop once and for all. 'But don't tell anyone at the chowk just yet, Aman bhai,' he pleaded. 'If they find out I'm finished.'

'I'll be sad to see you go, Kaka, but I don't think you have anything to worry about,' I replied. 'Everyone will miss you, but I'm sure we can find chai elsewhere.'

The next day I was to find out exactly how much everyone would miss Kaka if he left.

'Kaka owes me two thousand rupees, the bastard. He better not go anywhere,' said Lalloo in alarm, when I said that Kaka was looking unwell and casually suggested that the overworked chaiwallah go on holiday.

'Kaka owes *you* money?'

'Of course, Kaka owes us all money—except Ashraf of course. Ashraf has no money.'

'I always thought that you owed Kaka money.'

'That's only in the short term. In the long term, Kaka owes us.'

'How does Kaka have your money?'

'Well, I gave it to him! He'd better have it.'

I realized I had seriously misjudged Kaka's importance all these years. It's true that Kaka's tea was fractionally better than some of his competitors', but that was obviously not why everyone patronized him. Kaka wasn't just everyone's chaiwallah, he was everyone's banker!

Lalloo, Rehaan, everyone except for Ashraf, routinely dropped off a few hundred rupees with Kaka for safekeeping on the condition that he return the money on two or three days' notice. The system worked well as long as there were enough depositors and withdrawals were few: the mazdoors managed to save some money and Kaka received a substantial number of small, but useful, zero-interest loans that he invested in things like his son's soft drinks stand.

Lalloo's morning cup of tea was more than just a morning ritual; it was reassurance that his banker was hale, hearty, and solvent.

With the todh-phodh, work suddenly dried up and more and more mazdoors began asking for their money. Thus far, Kaka had managed to keep pace with the withdrawal, but the strain was beginning to tell. If word got out that Kaka was thinking of leaving, it would prompt a run on his bank—Kaka would never be able to pay off his loans fast enough and the mazdoors would lose all their savings.

I don't know why Kaka ever let on that he was thinking of leaving; it would have been so simple to pack up one night and never return. But where would he go? What would he do? And as Ashraf always said, you can't run all your life.

It takes years to build a clientele, and still more time to win their trust. Perhaps he was simply sending out a signal that he was in trouble too; that he needed some breathing space. The chaos of the todh-phodh continued till the end of the year, but the danger at Sadar Bazaar passed. Kaka stayed and honoured most of his debts.

four

AJNABI,
or Stranger

1

One morning, five years ago, Mohammed Ashraf forgot the phone number of the house where his mother lived.

For a long time, it was the only number he remembered. He would call her; she would ask him to come home. He would cry, she would cry. Then one day he forgot the number.

'I woke up one morning—drunk—and the number had slipped from my mind while I was asleep. It dribbled out of my open mouth; it escaped while I lay snoring. I asked Kaka if he remembered it; he was the one who punched it out for me. But his fingers forget the number the moment they press the buttons. They dial hundreds of numbers a day—how many numbers can they remember? Kaka says he only remembers his father's number.'

Ashraf thought of writing to her; but he had forgotten how to write. He tried a few words, but he kept getting confused with the matras, his hand started to hurt, and then he realized he had forgotten her address. The only address he remembered was 207 Patliputra Colony, Patna. But that was not her house—that was Dr Hussain's house. But even he didn't live there any more.

'I can remember roads; I'm brilliant at remembering roads. Once I walk along a read, I can always find my way back home. If I travel along a path more than once, I am almost certain to remember most major landmarks; and when there aren't any, I make my own. I remember the way to Grace Ma'am's house, I remember the way to school; but I don't know where my mother lives any more. She shifted after I left Patna.'

But he remembers the way to Raja's house. 'Remember Raja? Double BA Raja?' Even if you are a stranger to Calcutta, even today, after all these years, Ashraf can still tell you the way to Raja's; and if you make it there, he can tell you the way back home—if you still remember where you live, that is.

'When you get out of the Kalka Mail, it will be around seven o'clock in the morning, or maybe even eight. Sometimes protesters squat on the tracks, so count yourself lucky if you make it to Howrah by evening. Once out of the station, turn left. The Hooghly is on your right now, and you are walking up a road towards a gigantic steel cage of a bridge. You might recognize it from your childhood if you ever watched Doordarshan; they call it the Howrah Bridge—the new one.

'From the roundabout under the bridge catch the bus from Howrah to Sealdah—it's another railway station—and ride the bus from terminus to terminus all the way through Bara Bazaar. At the terminus keep the station on your right hand and walk on steadily past the bus depot towards the main chowk of Raja Bazaar.

'At the chowk you will see many labourers—just like us all here in Bara Tooti—but do not be distracted, turn right on to the bridge that goes to Narkul Danga. If anyone asks you, tell them you are looking for Raja's house: a small green house in the basti down this road.

'I never told you why Raja married twice. Before the second marriage Raja was a lafunter like me. It's impossible to find a house in Calcutta—at least a cheap house in a good location—and Raja could never save any money anyway. Whenever I put away a few notes, he would laugh—he was always laughing—and say, "Why? Ashraf bhai, why? We didn't come to Calcutta to build the fucking Taj Mahal."'

But Raja found his Mumtaz Begum and the Taj Mahal came for free. 'Now if only she would die like Mumtaz,' he would joke. 'Then I can bury her and grieve happily ever after.'

'But I think he likes her. These kinds of men like those kinds of women.'

'But why am I telling you about Raja again? How did we start this conversation? I remember now—I was telling you the way home from Raja's house. But for that I had to first tell you where his house was and then of course how he got the house. Funny how every short story is actually just the beginning of a really long one.

'Before he got the house we used to sleep together under the awning of the Momein Girls' High School. We had to wake up early before the schoolgirls came or the watchman would get angry and threaten to tell the police.'

For a week after Ashraf forgot his mother's address he didn't know what to do. He didn't know what it meant to be a complete lawaris without any fixed address, family, or home.

Kaka told him it was a good thing. 'There are lots of government schemes for lawaris people, Ashraf bhai. Free food, free medicines, free everything.' He said it was people like him—who had a house and a family—who were the worst off. 'Everyone thinks we are rich. But we are prisoners of our house—we can't sell it and we don't make enough money to live in it. Homeless lawaris people like you are completely free.'

But, one day he woke up and heard that the plumber in Bara Tooti, Ram Avatar, had died in his sleep and he understood. Lawaris meant he would die on a footpath in Delhi, and no one would even know.

'So what should we do, Ashraf bhai?'

'Let's go, Aman bhai, I think I'm ready.'

2

The loudspeaker crackles; the start-up jingle from an outdated version of Microsoft Windows echoes across the platforms of Old Delhi Railway Station. The woman with the metallic voice sings out the names and times of incoming trains.

Ashraf, Lalloo, and I stand outside the station, savouring one last chai together. I wanted to have tea at Kaka's stall—to bring things full circle in a way—but Ashraf wanted to get to the station on time. In a few minutes, Ashraf and I will hoist our bags onto our shoulders and make our way to the general compartment of the Howrah-bound Kalka Mail, and Lalloo will make the lonely walk back to Bara Tooti.

Ashraf's plan is to go back to Calcutta and rejoin Raja's floor polishing business. He is convinced that Raja will welcome him as a brother. He is ready to start over.

Without Ashraf, Lalloo isn't sure he wants to continue in the safedi business. He's never been to Calcutta, and says he would rather restart his paratha business in Delhi. Over the last few weeks, the three of us have worked out a budget for Ashraf and Lalloo. Ashraf reckons he needs about two thousand rupees: a thousand for the house—one month's deposit, one month's rent. Five hundred for tools, utensils, and other essentials, and another five hundred to keep him going for the first month.

Lalloo needs about the same: a thousand for the handcart, another five hundred for utensils, and the rest for vegetables, atta, salt, pickle. The money is a loan—Ashraf and Lalloo would never accept a favour of this scale—but it's a loan with a flexible repayment policy. 'I'm thinking of it as an investment,' I tell them. 'If you both do well, I shall have a stake in a paratha shop in Delhi and a thekedari in Calcutta.'

Ashraf and I will head to Calcutta. I'll stay a week, and when I return, Lalloo will be waiting with piping hot parathas from his stand. 'The first time you come, you can eat for free,' he offers, 'and as the business grows I'll pay you back.'

'We will always remember you, Aman bhai,' says Lalloo, as if he doubts I will ever come back. 'We won't forget you—especially how your sister went and helped poor Satish.'

In my five years at Bara Tooti, it is my sister's underwear purchase that has had the most resonance. Not that I admitted Satish into the hospital, or the hundreds of hours we spent together. No, all of that pales in comparison to the fact that my sister—a girl!—went into a TB ward to bring underwear for a man she had never met before. 'People like that are hard to find, Aman bhai.'

The woman with the metallic voice says something again. I think it's time. I stand up and walk off to smoke a cigarette and give the two of them some time by themselves.

'Chalo, Lalloo bhai, come to Calcutta sometime,' says Ashraf.

'Chalo, Ashraf bhai, make lots of money in Calcutta and return.'

I look back to see them embrace—Ashraf shaking with sobs, Lalloo consoling him.

•

The first hour passes in silence. Ashraf sits by the window, watching Delhi rush past. Once past Faridabad, the train picks up speed and Ashraf loosens up. 'I can't believe I'm leaving,' he says with a wry smile. 'For the last few months I was ekdum 100 per cent sure I would die in Delhi.'

We talk for a bit—random snippets of conversation as the train speeds through station after station. I smile my reassuring smile as often as I can; after breakfast I climb up onto the top berth and fall asleep.

I awake to sounds of raucous laughter. Ashraf and the Bengali bangle seller sitting across us are teasing the fifteen-year-old who is travelling home from Delhi for the first time.

'How do you know, how do you know?' says the youth defensively.

'Arre, don't you watch the movies? Ask anyone,' says Ashraf.

'He's going back to his village for the first time,' the bangle seller explains. 'He wants to prove to everyone he's become a big man.'

The boy looks crestfallen; he's still a child—maybe fifteen—who works at someone's house in Delhi. He's clearly proud of going back home with money in his pockets; it's the first vacation he's taken in two years. He has his cellphone charging next to him, he has a digital watch on his wrist.

'I got presents for everyone, but forgot about my sister-in-law. It's not such a big deal. But my brother just got married, so...'

'So he bought her something from the platform. Show us what you got? Show, show, show.'

The boy reaches into his bag and pulls out a slender necklace: it is a mangalsutra.

'Why didn't you buy your sister-in-law a wedding ring as well, you chootiya?' The bangle seller screeches with laughter. 'And some kumkum too.'

'What's her name? Draupadi?' asks Ashraf to more laughter.

'Now you tell me what to do.' The boy is distraught; he looks like he might cry.

Ashraf and his accomplice look penitent.

'I'll tell you what,' says the bangle seller. 'I'll give you a set of plain bangles—nothing too fancy—simple, colourful bangles that you can give your sister-in-law without upsetting your brother.'

'You are lucky you met such a good man,' says Ashraf sternly. 'Anyone else might have just let you go home and get slapped by your brother.'

The boy looks suitably grateful.

The train rolls on.

At night, Ashraf has slumped back into a surly silence. 'What if I can't find Raja?'

I reassure him as best as I can, but I am rather worried myself. The implications of our journey are slowly beginning to sink in. We have set off from Bara Tooti in search of a man that Ashraf last spoke to about fifteen years ago. That he has a house is reassuring, but what if Ashraf can't find him? I have booked return tickets, but the loss of face will probably kill Ashraf.

'There is no way I am returning to Bara Tooti,' he confirms. 'What will everyone say?'

The curse of the runaway is that he must return in materially superior circumstances. If you leave a mazdoor and return a mazdoor, then what have you achieved?

•

I'm chatting with the man on the side berth. We are discussing beards: his and mine.

'Are you Kashmiri?' he asks.

'No, are you?'

'No, no,' he says with a laugh. 'I'm from Calcutta, I saw your beard so I asked.'

'Same here,' I respond. It is hard not to see beards—affixed as they are to one's face. Mohammed Ijaz is one of those people who can look out of the window at any given point in a train journey and offer a precise speed–distance–time analysis of the journey.

'The train is running late,' he says glumly. 'My cows are waiting.'

He comes from a family of dairy farmers; they have about ten cows, each of which gives 'only best quality milk'. These days unscrupulous farmers mix chemicals with milk to make it appear creamier, but Ijaz's family has refrained from the practice.

'You must visit my uncle,' he says when I tell him we are going to Raja Bazaar. 'He makes the best tea in Calcutta, if not the entire country. It is the best tea shop in Raja Bazaar at least.' The secret is the tiny pinch of salt he puts into each cup. 'It brings the flavour out.'

3

It is a tiny room with plywood walls and a queen-sized bed. My feet stick out at the end. The bathroom and toilet are down the hall and shared between the six rooms on the second floor of Hotel Medina in Calcutta's Bara Bazaar. But it has a television and is only two hundred and fifty rupees for the night, so we take it.

We need to buy Ashraf a change of clothes—the canvas bag he has carried all the way from Delhi contains only a heavy shawl and a set of paint-splattered work clothes. He has gifted his brushes to Lalloo as he doesn't see himself working as a painter ever again. 'Raja mustn't think I have come begging for money. We will tell him that I am thinking of setting up a floor-polishing business in Calcutta and want his advice.'

So we drop our stuff off at the hotel and step out into Calcutta's Bara Bazaar.

'I want only solid colours,' says Ashraf. 'I don't like checks or stripes.' He also dislikes red, yellow, purple, black, electric lilac, ochre, and grey. He finally settles for two full-sleeved shirts: deep blue and dark green. Ashraf is a size 38.

Pants?

'No, Aman bhai, these are fine.' He dusts off his dark pants. 'There is only so much I can take from you.'

We get lunch at a dhaba—beef kababs and roti—and head back to the hotel. I fall asleep, Ashraf switches on the television.

I wake up to Mithun Chakraborty landing a crushing blow on a mortal enemy. I don't think Ashraf has blinked since he switched on the television. The man is obsessed. 'It's been ten years since I watched TV,' he confesses, 'and even then someone else had the remote.' We had left our door open and a small crowd comprising the cook, two errand boys, and the security guard has assembled to watch the movie. The guard has taken our chair and is sitting on it just outside our doorway.

'So what's the movie about?'

'Shush!' says the crowd, so I go back to sleep.

At six we head off to Raja Bazaar. Ashraf does indeed have an amazing head for roads. Guided solely by memory, he cuts through alleyways to arrive at the precise cut in the road where Bara Bazaar merges into Raja Bazaar.

The Raja Bazaar chowk is deserted when we arrive, except for a solitary paanwallah who is shutting down for the day.

'I'm looking for Raja mota—Raja, the fat one.'

'He's probably at his house—you know it?'

'The one near the Momein Girls' High School?'

'Yes, the same. Wait, Ashraf?'

'Yes, it's me,' says Ashraf, completely unfazed by the fact that this man remembers him after all these years.

'I thought so. You've lost weight.'

•

Once over the flyover, Ashraf drops me off at Ijaz's uncle's tea shop. I finally taste his world-famous tea; it's...milky. The cup of tea and a samosa later, Ashraf arrives with a middle-aged man dressed in a vest and lungi. Raja is short, fat, balding, and smokes cigarettes rather than beedis.

We talk briefly, Raja assures us that he is thrilled to see us, but the words seem forced, the gaiety burdened. Ashraf and Raja appear uncomfortable, like distant relatives who can't quite place each other.

'The floor-polishing business is over,' declares Raja. 'Now it's all machines and contractors. But don't worry, Ashraf, we'll find something for you.'

The distance between them isn't lost on either. Raja is the successful businessman who owns two houses, has put two sons through school, and no longer has to work for a living. He prattles on, talking about his sons who have moved to Bombay and are starting businesses of their own, even as Ashraf appears smaller and smaller. He is far away now, lost in the starched creases of his new blue shirt—Ashraf, who has returned with nothing.

He's quiet on his way back to the hotel. Raja has offered to take him house hunting in the morning. 'He said, "I can't let you stay with me. Please understand, Ashraf, I have a wife now." It's fine, I will start something on my own. I don't need Raja any more.'

We come back to find the hotel staff have unlocked our room with the skeleton key and are sitting just outside the doorway, watching TV. Ashraf takes the remote from the security guard (who is sitting on our chair); I throw a blanket over my head and fall asleep.

The muezzin calls the faithful to prayer at five in the morning. Ashraf and I awake and find a tea shop that has just opened up. The bitterness of last evening has dissolved, Ashraf appears hopeful. 'It is better this way. Once I have my house, maybe my mother can come and visit me. She can stay for a few months, help me set up house, find me a wife.'

'How will you find her, Ashraf?'

'I have relatives in Calcutta; they might know where she is.'

'Relatives? Can we meet them?'

'Not yet. Once I have a running business, and a few more shirts—maybe next time you visit Calcutta. Don't get distracted, Aman bhai, today we must find my house. All this interview-baazi for your book can come later.'

This morning, Raja appears close to expressing genuine warmth. He is reconciled to the fact that Ashraf is here to stay. 'I keep telling Ashraf bhai not to worry,' he says conspiratorially while Ashraf has gone to buy some beedis. 'We are all here to look after him.'

'Ashraf, are you sure you can trust these guys?' Ashraf and I are squeezed together at the back in a local train. Raja and an associate are standing by the open door, smoking cigarettes. Ashraf nods silently. Shorn of his Delhi swagger, Ashraf is a worried man: unsure, tentative, and at the mercy of a man who has changed a great deal since the time he called Ashraf his closest friend.

The house is going to cost us six hundred rupees a month. It's a straw hut about an hour outside Calcutta, with nothing—not even an electricity connection—but Raja insists it's the cheapest option. 'Stay here for a few months and maybe later you can find something better.'

Ashraf looks to me for advice; I can tell he is getting pinned into a corner. I can put down money for the first month, but there is no way he can afford a place like this. 'What do you think, Aman bhai?'

'I don't know, Ashraf bhai, you tell me. Do you think you will manage?'

'I'll take it,' he says simply, his voice low and nervous. 'If I can't manage, I'll find another place.'

On the train journey back Raja tries to sell Ashraf a set of used tools 'at a special discount rate. A friend of mine no longer wants them, they are as good as new.' Ashraf beats him back, Raja sulks all the way back to the bazaar.

Raja invites us over to his house, 'to celebrate Ashraf bhai's return', but Ashraf declines. 'Come,' he says, taking my hand in his, 'let's go home and watch TV.'

Ashraf wakes up early next morning—his eyes burnt red by the TV screen—and drags me downstairs for a chai and cigarette before he leaves to look for work at the Raja Bazaar chowk. 'Might as well start as a safediwallah,' he says. 'Then I'll see if anything good comes along.'

We sit at the same tea shop as yesterday. Ashraf tells me a story about a house he once painted where the home owner was a holy man who had six students—each of whom turned out to be a ghost. I tell him about the time I interviewed a gangster who had a soft spot for badminton. We both pack our bags, and Ashraf sets off towards the market. 'I'll spend the first night at the chowk, and maybe move to the house tomorrow.'

I leave the hotel at noon and go down to Park Street, buy a book and have my first decent cup of coffee in a week. I check my email at an internet café, bump into an old college acquaintance, and have lunch.

Ashraf calls as I am boarding my train, his voice already sounding like he is far away. We exchange notes, I offer him advice, he assures me he will be careful—particularly around Raja. He asks me to give his love to everyone at Bara Tooti; I assure him I will.

And then he tells me a story.

4

She was sixteen when he married her. It was a union borne out of circumstance. When he looked back at the time in which it was formalized, it almost seemed like an elaborate conspiracy hatched by the Almighty.

He had told his mother he was not interested in marriage, much less in marrying someone from her immediate family, and certainly not the daughter of a first cousin. 'But that makes you second cousins,' she countered. 'A second cousin is twice removed.' But despite his protests, he did accompany his mother to her cousin's house to look at the girl, and he did look into her eyes and smile when the girl offered him tea and a plate of glucose biscuits.

He spent the length of the overnight train ride home convincing his mother of the unsuitability of this match.

'Does her mother know what I do?'

'She knows you, my son, that you have done some schooling, and that you can support a family, and that is enough.'

'But does she know what I do now?'

'You are running a successful business; why should you be ashamed?'

'Her mother will object.'

'So let her.'

In the end, he did succeed in buying more time.

'Our son is still young,' dictated his mother to the letter writer who sat under a balcony in the main bazaar. 'Though by god's grace his business is growing rapidly, he still needs a year to establish himself. I wish your daughter the very best.'

But the girl was still unmarried a year later; her mother was still interested, and, much to his annoyance, so was his. Arguments at home followed a familiar script of him explaining how he was not ready for so grave a commitment, and his mother gently sobbing about the years she had worked tirelessly to bring up her three children. 'What about me?' she asked. 'Don't I deserve even a little rest in my old age?'

The matter was finally resolved by the untimely, yet well-timed, death of his elder sister in childbirth. She left behind three young boys who were promptly disowned by her husband who had always been a good-for-nothing anyway. Exhausted by her years of child rearing, his mother threw up her hands at the prospect of raising another three children. What was required was a young bride who would uncomplainingly fulfil her household duties.

And so a date was fixed, a ceremony conducted, and a marriage solemnized. As he had predicted, her mother was horrified to learn—'Far too late,' as she was fond of saying—that her daughter was being married off to a mere butcher, and with his mother maintaining that the girl was lucky to be married at all, the marriage started on a fractious note. The poor girl was also horrified to realize that she was, at the age of seventeen, expected to look after a household that comprised not just a controlling mother-in-law and a boisterous brother-in-law, but three young, wailing children as well. She often ran home to her mother's place in Calcutta, and he would arrive home after work—smelling of blood, guts, and meat—to find an absent wife and an enraged mother. 'Bring her home,' she would scream, even as she struggled to feed the three orphaned boys. 'Filthy butcher,' his mother-in-law would shout when he showed up hot, sweaty, and tired after the night-long train journey. 'How did I ever let my daughter marry such a man?'

It is true that it was a gory job, but certainly not one to attract the kind of contempt displayed by his mother-in-law. It was his business; he had built it the old-fashioned way— starting from scratch with a minuscule punji and building it up day by day till he was doing several hundred rupees worth of business every day. It wasn't a fortune, but it was enough to run a family in some comfort. He liked to see himself as a businessman in the meat and chicken line, but to his mother-in-law he was always a filthy butcher.

She would relent after a few hours and let her daughter return; he, for his part, would promise to treat her better and look after her every need. 'She will never feel any lack of anything ever again,' he would declare, but a few months later she would run away once more.

In time, however, they began to understand each other, and then one day he could say, with some honesty, that they were in love. Not a heady, overpowering passion, but a quiet and tender love that was cemented by the birth of a chubby girl followed by a skinny boy three years later.

Knowing that her mother disapproved of her husband, his wife attempted to placate her by surreptitiously sending money to prove how well he was doing. After a few months of missing his money, he caught her taking it out of his work shirt. No amount of explaining could recover the situation. He accused her of trying to ruin his business—'Because your mother never approved of it anyway.' She tried to explain, but gave up when she realized that the love, so carefully built on compromise, was irrevocably lost. The next day he came home drunk for the first time, after which it was only a matter of time till she left for her mother's place once more.

This time she took their children along. This time he refused to fetch her. Two months later he received a letter from his mother-in-law informing him that another, more suitable husband had been found for her daughter. The man was a rich widower who had agreed to look after the children. After eight years of marriage, Mohammed Ashraf sold off his business, paid off his debts, and tied his belongings into a large cloth bundle. Whatever money remained he handed over to his mother, and left on the first Delhi-bound train that arrived at Patna Station.

'But when did you find the time to get married, Ashraf bhai?'

'Between Bombay and Delhi. I told you I went home to Patna for a while.'

'By a while I thought you meant a few months. Not eight years. What happened to the children?'

'I don't know. I never saw them again.'

'Do you think of them often?'

'No, just sometimes.'

•

Dear Aman bhai,

God willing this letter finds you and your family safe
and sound. Here in Calcutta, I am working hard and
doing well. Unlike Delhi, there is plenty of work here
in Calcutta, especially for painters like me. There are
not so many safediwallahs in Calcutta.

The next time you go to Bara Tooti, can you please
buy me some paintbrushes—they are much cheaper in
Delhi. Here, it is almost five hundred rupees a brush.
Lalloo will know which brushes to buy.

Please give my love to your parents and sister.

Your brother,
Ashraf

The blue inland letter lay on my desk for many days. It
was swept up with the trash and retrieved; three months
after I received it, I finally wrote to Ashraf.

Dear Ashraf bhai,

Sorry for this late reply to your letter. I have been
travelling and couldn't find the time. I haven't bought
the brushes since I don't know how to send them
to you. Nonetheless, we can go shopping when I
next visit Calcutta. I am happy that you have found
work. Please keep working hard and try not to drink
too much.

Write back once you get this. My family sends their
love.

Aman Sethi

Inshallah, we will meet soon in Calcutta,

Your brother,
Aman

Ashraf never wrote back but a year later I visited Calcutta. I was leaving to spend the year in New York, the book was nearly complete, and I wanted to meet him before I left.

5

I couldn't find Hotel Medina, but found something similar in the vicinity of the main mosque for two hundred rupees a night. This time there is no television, and no Ashraf, but I wake up early with the call to prayer and walk down to the same chaiwallah and smoke a cigarette in solitude.

I am tempted to talk to Raja about Ashraf's wife. Raja is one of Ashraf's oldest friends; with his help, it would be easy to track her down. But should I?

I often toy with the idea of verifying Ashraf's stories. Maybe make a trip down to Patna to 207 Patliputra Colony to see if it really existed, if Dr Hussain had ever lived there. Maybe search for Taneja's shop on Exhibition Street.

But why should I? How would that change anything between us, except convince Ashraf that I mistrust him and that his story is more important to me than he is?

But his wife can probably give me an insight into a certain phase of Ashraf's life that no one else can. I decide not to ask Raja, but to gently suggest to Ashraf that I might be interested in interviewing his wife. If he freaks out, I will drop the subject forever.

I do not have an address or a number, but I find Raja Bazaar quite easily and Raja's house is just down the road from there. Raja has grown fatter and lost some more hair, but I recognize him sleeping on a charpai outside his house. Moments after we order the mandatory cup of tea, it is apparent that he and Ashraf aren't talking any more.

Ashraf is selfish and ungracious and refuses to acknowledge everything that Raja has done for him. He assumed that Raja owed him a favour simply because he had left him half the stone-polishing business twenty years ago. 'That business is dead, I sold it off ten years ago. There is no stone polishing any more. Everyone has machines.'

Just because he has come from Delhi, Ashraf thinks he's better than everyone else, and finally, he drinks too much and curses loudly when he does, and as a respectable man with a wife and family, Raja simply cannot tolerate it.

He pauses for a breath. When Ashraf fell ill, Raja had spent hundreds, no, a few thousand rupees, to get him medicines, but Ashraf refused to repay him. Now Ashraf has run off to Tangra and Raja never wants to see him again.

How can I find him?

'I don't know. But he has started drinking again—at Debiji's vend near the Goru Kilkhana. Ask around there.'

Debiji's theka is not the seedy desi sharab shack I had expected; it turns out to be a red multi-storeyed house with a handsome nameplate announcing its owners. Debiji is not the proprietor of a liquor vend; she is a wholly respectable married lady, who fortunately isn't home when I arrive.

'Debiji's' is an illegal operation run out of the basement by her useless younger brothers—Prabhu and Veeru—who buy illegally distilled alcohol and sell it for a fraction of the market price of licensed liquor. Ashraf had become close friends with the brothers and with his voracious appetite for alcohol, is, I can imagine, presenting them with a bit of a golden goose problem.

He is, by far, their best customer, one who can quite happily spend an entire week's earnings in a night of heavy drinking; but the more he drinks, the less money he earns.

'I never let Ashraf drink too much,' says Prabhu, a thin, reedy man with a liking for solemn declarations. 'Just one glass in the mornings when he picks up his tools and a bit in the evenings after work. I tell him he has to stay in control.'

To safeguard their client's interests, they even keep his tools in their shop overnight—lest they be stolen from the pavement where he sleeps.

Ashraf himself has aged considerably in the past year. His movements have lost some of their fluidity; his hands tremble as he takes his beedi to his mouth. 'I'm a bit ill, Aman bhai,' he says with an apologetic smile. 'How did you find me?'

The grin is gone the moment I bring up Raja's name: Raja is selfish and ungracious and refuses to acknowledge everything that Ashraf has done for him. Of course, the business is dead now, but while it was running, it had put Raja's children through school, built him a second house, and made him into the kind of old, fat zamindar that everyone hated.

It is true that Raja spent about a thousand rupees when Ashraf fell ill—but he got the money by selling Ashraf's complete set of tools without his permission. What tools they were: a large, heavy hammer with a perfectly weighted head, two broad brushes, four smaller brushes, scrapers, a majula, a plumb line—everything. They were worth at least two thousand rupees. Raja must have spent the rest of the money on himself, and still had the temerity to ask Ashraf for more.

Now, Ashraf coughs theatrically. After a year of hard work, Ashraf is exactly where he started: sleeping on the pavement with no money, and no tools.

And his uncles, did he finally visit them?

Just once and they refused to help. He spent twenty rupees getting his clothes washed and ironed, ten rupees on bus fare, and another fifty rupees on a box of sweets. The kindly old uncle was dead, and Ashraf's cousins were fearful of giving him a share of their business.

And his mother?

His mother is dead. Well, not really. Well, actually he has no idea where she is. He assumes she would be dead by now. She was quite old.

'I don't think I will ever see her again, so she's as good as dead,' he concludes in his typically logical fashion.

I ask him if I could talk to his ex-wife. He refuses. Later in the evening we go out for a walk and he tells me that Prabhu and Veeru used to be very successful businessmen till one batch of rum went horribly wrong and fourteen people died. 'They sold everything they had to get the enquiry hushed up.'

No, it doesn't bother him that the same two men now sell him two bottles of alcohol a day. 'It wasn't their fault; it could happen to anybody.'

•

On my last day, we set out to buy Ashraf a new set of tools—he wants a change from the safedi line.

'Bengalis don't care to paint their houses,' he says with a sniff. 'They are the shabbiest people I know.'

He wants to become a santrash—a specialized line of mazdoors who break houses rather than build them. 'There is a system for everything in Calcutta,' he says. 'One line of people build, another set break, another set paint—everything is very organized.'

'So is there a specific technique for breaking houses?'

'Of course there is. There is a specific technique for everything.'

'So what is it? You start from a particular wall...or...?'

'You start from the roof, Aman bhai. If you break the walls first, you'll get buried by the roof. You really can be very stupid at times.'

The santrash line traces its lineage back to court sculptors and anyone who worked with a hammer and a chisel.

'There is a lot of work for santrashes in Calcutta: cutting air-conditioning ducts, making openings for exhaust fans, thin channels for laying electrical wiring, thick channels for water pipes.

'The santrash line is a risky line. All sorts of things are released when you break a wall—dreams, desires, secrets...'

I like the idea of a house absorbing what occurs within the safety of its four walls: sound waves imprinting themselves onto wet concrete surfaces like a phonograph record to be read by the santrash's hammer.

Ashraf natters on as we take the bus from Raja Bazaar to a part of Calcutta called Dharamtala. It's a short ride but the bus makes many stops. As we step off near Calcutta's large, open maidan, a man brushes against me and vanishes into the crowd. Instinctively, my hand reaches for my back pocket—my wallet is missing.

Ashraf takes the news rather well—certainly far better than I do.

'Don't worry, Aman bhai. Look, I have seven rupees in my pocket. Let's get some tea and think—I'll pay.'

We get tea. I smoke a cigarette: the wallet has my credit cards, my press card, and a significant amount of money. Worryingly, I still have to pay for my hotel and buy Ashraf his tools.

'Don't worry about the tools, Aman bhai, this happens to me all the time. Wake up feeling like I am going to conquer the world, only to be stabbed in the back.'

If only the staff at the hotel prove to be so understanding. I'm having visions of leaving my watch at the reception, promising to wire them money. Maybe they will tut-tut sympathetically and say that these things happen. Maybe my wallet shall miraculously reappear in my bag. I suddenly realize I don't really know anyone at all in this city; my sole friend from Calcutta now works in Bombay.

'So what are you going to do?'

'I don't know. I think I'm going to call my mom.'

Ten minutes later, it's all done. My parents have righted the balance of my world. The brother of a family friend has been located. He will be at a gathering of dentists at lunchtime at Trincas on Park Street. 'Uncle will give you six thousand rupees,' says my mother reassuringly. 'Enough for your hotel bill and Ashraf's tools.'

It's only 11:30, but I can wait. Ashraf looks on as I call my bank to cancel my cards. Twenty minutes later that's done too.

'Do you have any more money, Ashraf? I really need a cigarette.'

'Let me check.'

A crumpled ten-rupee note has emerged from a secret pocket in his trousers' waistband. 'I had forgotten all about it. Maybe I have some more money elsewhere.' Ashraf smiles as he frisks himself for cash. 'Let's get you a cigarette and some tea.'

•

'I was just thinking, Aman bhai, what would you have done if you didn't have a phone?'

'I'd probably ask someone if I could use their phone.'

'What if you didn't have that option? If your mother didn't know someone in Calcutta? If no one knew anyone?'

'I don't know, Ashraf bhai. I'd probably go to the police and ask for help.'

'Basically you would beg for help, wouldn't you, Aman bhai? Just like the rest of us. Your level is a little higher—so you could go begging to the police. Our level is a little lower...'

'So where would you go?'

'To Jamil bhai.'

Jamil bhai, later to become Jamil saab, was a great man.

For a period in the 1980s, or so Ashraf says, he ruled the beedi-rolling trade in Calcutta. Every beedi produced in Calcutta was rolled by his workers, slipped into paper packets bearing the insignia of various brands, and shipped out to the rest of the country.

In later years, he handed over control to his sons and went about setting up the entire stretch of shops from the Raja Bazaar main road down towards Narkul Danga.

'Jamil saab was like us; he came out of Raja Bazaar when there wasn't much of a bazaar to speak of. All this is before my time, but I heard that one day Jamil saab got all the people living in Raja Bazaar together and asked them to dip their hands into a cloth bag and pull out a chit. Jamil saab then looked at every chit and said, "You, you will become a butcher and sell chicken. You will open a vegetable shop; you will sell milk." On and on he went, telling everyone what they should do. Then he gave everyone some money to start their shops and told them to buy their things and start immediately.'

It seems that for some years he took rent from everyone, but later he made so much money that he even stopped doing that. In a manner faintly reminiscent of the freeing of slaves, Ashraf claims Jamil called everyone out one day. (In Ashraf's narrative Jamil saab was always calling people out into a gathering to hear his latest diktat.) He said, 'You are free now. As long as I am alive no one will ask you for any rent or hafta or donation or anything.' And no one did.

Soon after, Jamil saab retired to a house in South Calcutta and dedicated himself to doing good works. He would come to his office in Raja Bazaar for a few hours every day to hold court, listen to complaints, redress wrongs.

A lot of mazdoors would go to him at festival time. 'They would say a pickpocket stole their money and train ticket and they were left with nothing. Jamil saab would listen and ask one or two questions. Only one or two questions.' Ashraf is insistent on the precise nature of the interrogation.

'He would only ask, "Where are you from? Where were you going to? And how much was the ticket?" and from just those three questions, he would be able to tell if you were lying!'

'Exactly how?'

'Because Jamil saab knew the exact rail fares between any two stations. See, in the railways, it's all a formula.' I've started Ashraf off on the railways again. 'The fare is based on the distance—and Jamil saab knew the distance to everywhere, so automatically he knew the fare.'

As Ashraf would put it, 'It really is very simple.' If Jamil saab believed you, he would call up his most trusted munshi—from Ashraf's description, a sad little man with nothing to do except book train tickets—and ask him to buy the mazdoor a ticket on the next train. 'Sometimes, he would even give the mazdoor a little extra money for the journey.'

'So did you ever need to go to Jamil saab, Ashraf bhai?'

'No, I didn't, but I knew several people who did. But now he's gone.'

According to Ashraf, there are Jamil-like figures in every major city—except Delhi. Bombay, for instance, has the Ghanswallahs. 'They are an old Parsi family. I think their forefathers sold horse fodder to the British. They also give money to mazdoors to go home.'

I observe that no one gives money for people to come to cities—only to go back home.

Ashraf nods his head; we sit back in the maidan and wait for lunchtime and its promise of money.

•

We are looking for a workshop from where to buy a good hammer and a set of chennis—metal picks of various sizes and strength to cut holes in brick, plaster, and concrete surfaces. Hammers are relatively easy to come by, but you can't buy a chenni off the shelf.

The meeting with my father's friend's brother had gone surprisingly well—notwithstanding my dishevelled appearance. 'Best of luck, son,' he said gravely as he gave me his number. 'Any further troubles, just call.'

Six thousand rupees tucked into my jeans (how I wish I had a secret pocket) I slipped out into the street where Ashraf was waiting, and together we headed off to Dharamtala.

'The best chennis are made from the suspension coils of old model Ambassador cars,' says the blacksmith as he bangs away on his anvil. 'The only problem is you can't find any scrap any more. China is buying everything. Old cars, spare parts, spoons, plates, ships—anything made of metal that you drop into a dustbin gets sorted, packed, and shipped off to China. Same with suspension coils. How will India become great if we keep selling everything to the Chinese?'

A good chenni must be absolutely straight to transmit the force of the hammer into the wall. Any kinks and the chenni will snap when you strike it too hard.

Ashraf selects a few pieces and as the blacksmith straightens them out tells me how he is fighting a case against the Uttar Pradesh government for removing him from his post as a homoeopathic healer in a government hospital. 'I have come up with a pioneering cure for cancer,' says the blacksmith. 'But I can only tell you about it once I have the time to file for a patent. You have to be very careful. How can we make India great if we keep stealing each other's ideas?'

6

'You could say nothing has changed, Aman bhai, and then again everything has changed. No one has changed, but everyone has changed.'

Looking at Kaka, it's hard to imagine that only five years have passed since I started coming to Bara Tooti. I've been away in the US for one of those years, and in that time—the gulf that I had so assiduously bridged—seems to have widened again. I've forgotten many names, many faces have forgotten me. It's eight in the morning, but the crowd seems to have abandoned Kaka's. A year after the financial crisis obliterated any chances I had of finding a job in New York, have the mazdoors of Bara Tooti finally lost faith in their banker as well?

'You have certainly changed, Kaka,' I say. 'For one, you have become even fatter.'

'Don't make fun of an old man, Aman bhai. I think I have diabetes.'

'Must be all that sugar in your tea, Kaka. Where is everybody?'

'Haven't you heard? Do you remember this man called Sunil, Aman bhai? Thin fellow with wispy brown hair, moustache but no beard—never drank, never smoked, never took ganja? Sunil found a thekedari on the Sonipat side near a place called Rai. A short assignment of maybe three or four days; a factory needed to be painted.'

'They all went—Rehaan, Naushad, Kale Baba, Munna. The factory sent an open van and they set off like schoolchildren on a class trip to the local Coca-Cola factory.

'Well, this was more a warehouse than a factory—with those high, double ceilings. So Munna and Kale Baba lashed the ladders together and reinforced them with double knots. Rehaan climbed up and was putting primer on the exhaust grilles. He was right on top; maybe two storeys up when—I don't quite know what happened—the ladder slipped.'

The body is breakable. The body with its puffed-out chest, its tight, rope-like biceps, its dense, bulging calves. The body that can scramble up walls, balance on pillars, and drag a loaded handcart up three flights of stairs. Dropped off a tall ladder, these bones shatter, these muscles tear, these tendons snap, and when they do, they leave behind a crumpled shell in the place of a boy as beautiful and agile as Rehaan.

He was rushed to a nearby hospital where he was in a coma for almost a week. Munna found a small black diary in his breast pocket and called his family. They came down on the fourth day after the accident. He died on the seventh without ever regaining consciousness.

'Remember Naushad, Rehaan's friend? Maybe you never spoke with him, but he and Rehaan used to smoke together all the time. Two days after Rehaan's accident, Naushad was leaning over the side of the factory's terrace, putting a base coat on a ledge. His elbow nudged the pot of paint, he leaned out further to save it, and fell six storeys to his death. No one even knew who to call, and you wouldn't have recognized his body anyway.'

'What about Kale Baba?'

The old man whose skin was leathery, whose hair was so wiry, whose beard was so crusty that it was impossible to imagine a site at which even the most persistent of infections could take root. The old man who made eighty thousand rupees when his brothers gave him a share of their shop, but drank it away in less than eighty days.

'They used to say that even death couldn't kill Kale Baba, but he died on this trip too. Some say it was pneumonia, but Lalloo says it was heartbreak.'

'Lalloo's here? Did he finally restart his paratha business?'

'Ah, Lalloo. We hadn't seen him for three days and then one morning I found him sleeping on the main road near the chowk. I called out his name; I shouted, "Lalloo, Lalloo," and he awoke with a start and ran at me with madness in his eyes. He picked up a brick and hit me on the forehead.'

At the chowk, they say he ran down Teli Bara Road to Kalyani's and asked for the thousand rupees he had given her for safekeeping. He tried to buy some Everyday, but she refused so he swore at her and ran off towards the railway station.

Three days later, some boys from Bara Tooti were riding home in a thekedar's tempo when they saw a naked man running along Sadar Thana Road chasing cycle rickshaws. They shouted, 'Lalloo, Lalloo,' but he kept running, his fists full of money, screaming, 'Two hundred rupees for the day. Today I want to see all of Delhi, everything. Five hundred, six hundred, seven hundred for the day.' They tried to get the truck to stop, but they were stuck in the back and the driver in the cab couldn't hear them. They said they could hear his voice all the way to Bara Tooti: 'Eight hundred, nine hundred, ten thousand rupees for a cycle ride around Delhi.'

No one ever saw the body. The chikwallahs on Idgah Road told Munna that the police had found a scarred, naked body of a forty-something man who had a steel rod in his leg. His opened fist still had some money in it. There was froth around his mouth. The police took the body and put it in the morgue at Baraf Khana.

They said he died of pagalpan—madness.

7

'I'm looking for a man called Mohammed Ashraf.'

The attendant, sprawled out on the wooden bench, sits up and rubs his eyes.

'This is the Bihari Ashraf?'

'Yes, I was told he is a patient here.'

'Bed 32, Narayani Ward, second floor.'

A year on, Ashraf has been diagnosed with multi-drug-resistant tuberculosis, or MDR, as everyone in Narayani Ward at the K.S. Rai TB Hospital in Jadavpur terms it. He was diagnosed in September last year and has since spent the past ten months at the hospital.

I spot him on the balcony; he's in a clean lungi and a thin cotton vest. He's lost a lot of muscle on his arms, but ten months of regular meals have given him a rather substantial paunch.

'Sit, sit, sit.' He wipes the wooden bench he is sitting on and pulls up a chair. A face mask dangles freely around his neck; he pulls it on, but then takes it off as he starts talking. 'Where have you been? How was America? How did you find me? It's so good to see you.'

'How are you?' I ask, my questions excitedly tumbling over Ashraf's. 'How long have you been here? America was okay. I called up Prabhu the bootlegger. He told me you had TB. I'm so glad I found you.'

The doctors have told me not to stay beyond twenty minutes and to keep my face turned away at all times. But it's hard to look away and set a time limit while talking to Ashraf.

'Soon after you left for America, I began to wake up coughing. I ignored it, but it got worse and worse. So I stopped smoking. But it wouldn't stop. So I stopped drinking, but it still continued.

'By then Prabhu and Veeru were also getting a little worried. I went to the doctor. I thought, might as well get treatment and go to my death well-dressed and prepared.'

Multi-drug-resistant TB is the ghost of Indian TB programmes past. The earliest cases of drug resistance were noted in 1947 when the TB bacteria displayed a worrying resistance to streptomycin, the first antibiotic treatment for tuberculosis. By the 1960s, strains of the bacteria had developed resistance to newer drugs like Isoniazid; and by the late 1990s, the bacteria had got the better of Rifampicin, a semi-synthetic antibiotic expressly used to fight the disease. A primary cause for the resistance, according to medical journals, was that patients did not complete the full course of their medication—in effect, serving as living, breathing petri dishes for more and more virulent strains of the disease.

'The problem with the patient is that the bacteria are

lodged deep inside the tissue,' said Dr T. Bannerjee. 'His tests will come back negative, but in the X-ray we can see the bacteria eating away at his lungs.' Dr Bannerjee was a slight, neatly dressed Bengali gentleman with a fondness for checked shirts in varying shades of brown. He had a clipped moustache and his hair was arranged around a razor-sharp side parting. Years of interviewing TB patients had trained Dr Bannerjee to sit as far behind his desk as he possibly could, and to face his subject as infrequently as possible. My meeting was conducted entirely in side profile, Dr Bannerjee shooting me quick glances from the corner of his eye as he spoke of Ashraf's predicament. 'I hope you can convince him to stay for the full treatment. The MDR drugs are highly toxic and patients like him, with no one to encourage them, often drop out once the symptoms disappear.'

On Bed 32 in Narayani Ward, Ashraf insists he will complete the course. 'I should complete at least one course of one thing in my life,' he remarks.

But the medicines are lethal. 'Your face changes,' says Kedarnath Misra, the taxi driver on Bed 29. 'The day someone starts the MDR treatment, everyone in the ward can tell just by looking at him.'

The first week is the worst: every part of the body feels like it is on fire, 'like an acid eating you up from the inside'. Not many patients can handle the toxicity. They can walk, they can move, but they can't eat without vomiting up everything forced down their throats. Now in its second month, Kedarnath's body has grown accustomed to the medicine searing through his veins. 'It still burns—but in a different way; in a way like I can feel it killing the disease inside me.'

'The drug is like an electric shock to the brain,' says Ashraf. 'One shot and you are finished—ekdum khatam.'

•

The next day, I bring along a game of Ludo. Ashraf, Kedarnath from Bed 29, and Mustafa from Bed 31 put their masks in place and gather around on Ashraf's bed.

'We wouldn't want you to get TB,' says Ashraf. 'That would be very sad.'

Ashraf plays red, I play yellow. Mustafa plays green—but he cheats when he throws the dice. As the game goes on, we talk about life in the hospital. The drugs have eaten away Ashraf's muscles—his arms look weak and flabby; he says he can't raise them above the shoulder. For a santrash, this is a serious problem.

The tools we bought last year are safe in Prabhu's theka, but he's unlikely to ever use them again. He could sell them, or rent them out at two rupees a chenni a day, but he can't live off that money. 'I'm thinking of starting a sabzi ka business. Buy seasonal vegetables from the villages near Calcutta and sell them in the city every day. I did that for some time as a child—sometimes lemons, sometimes lauki, tomatoes.'

He seems wistful and far away. He speaks often of death, how it's hard to stay sane when everyone has relatives who visit, friends who bring food, wives and daughters and sons and brothers who drop by. 'My daughter's name was Shabnam,' he says suddenly. 'I've forgotten my son's name—he was barely a year old. I don't know who to live for any more, Aman bhai. There is nothing but sorrow in this hospital. I try to distract myself, but all I can think of is a day when I will try to wake up and won't.'

'Think of Kalyani and her high-waisted petticoats. The way she used to lean especially low when she filled your glass. The way she would say "Ashraaaaf bhaaaai" and pout.'

'I had a real chance with her, no?' He's grinning now. 'She used to give so much lift. I should have done something. But interest nahi tha.'

'What about in Calcutta?'

'Here and there. There was this woman I met in Tangra. I was drinking chai and she came up to me and pretended she knew me from before.'

'You knew her?'

'Arre, I didn't know who she was; but what she was I could tell with my eyes closed. I said I have no money and no room; she had a room and offered me a special rate.'

'What rate?'

'See, first time, I think she just really wanted to have sex. So it was free, because she wanted.

'Second time, we just met at the market by accident. I wasn't really in the mood, but I didn't mind having sex with her, and she was really sweet, and she didn't mind having sex with me. So we had sex araam se, and I paid her thirty rupees.

'Third time, I really wanted to have sex with her—I went specifically to look for her near the chai shop and so she charged me forty-five rupees. After that I got tuberculosis.

'But she really liked me, you know. The normal rate is at least seventy rupees.'

'So have you met her since?'

'I sneaked out once to Ghutiyar Market.'

'Does she know you have TB?'

'These things you don't tell people, Aman bhai. Even once you get cured.'

His loneliness has convinced Ashraf of the need to marry again. 'At least someone will come to see me if I fall ill again, or something happens.' He notices me smiling to myself. 'I still get offers, Aman bhai,' he says stiffly. 'There are lots of women who couldn't get married because of money problems and so their marriage age expired. Once my vegetable business takes off, the offers will come pouring in.'

'What about Delhi,' he asks suddenly. 'How is everyone? Has Lalloo started his paratha business?'

And so I tell him. He takes the news quietly, discreetly wiping away tears from the corner of his eye. 'Lalloo should have come to Calcutta with me. We could have taken care of each other. Chalo, everyone has to go when their time comes. Today it is Lalloo, tomorrow it could be me—who knows? I'm the last one left, Aman bhai. Everyone else is gone: Satish, Lalloo, Rehaan. But I'm still here, in a TB hospital. Dreaming of marriage; and I'm not even all that old.'

'How old are you, Ashraf bhai? It's been five years and we still haven't finished our timeline.' I pull out my notebook one last time.

8

1 August 1966—Mohammed Ashraf is born to Sakina in Guraru in Gaya, Bihar. His father works for the railways near Patna, but Ashraf has no memories of him.

1968—Ashraf's younger brother Mohammed Aslam is born.

1971—Ashraf's father dies, leaving Sakina with the two boys and a tiny piece of land that she farms and subsequently leases out.

1975—Ashraf is in Patna; he knows this because he remembers the floods of 1975 when the city was submerged for three days. They were living in a jhuggi somewhere on the outskirts of Patna, clinging onto their mother and praying they wouldn't drown.

1976—Mohammed Ashraf, aged ten, comes to Dr Hussain's house.

December 1984—Dr Hussain is attacked by Taneja's goons and dies a few weeks later.

January 1985—Ashraf moves to Calcutta with his mother and younger brother Aslam.

1987—Ashraf marries for the first and only time. Worried that I might track his wife down, he still refuses to give me her name.

1990—Aslam stabs someone. Ashraf, his wife, and his family move back to Patna. Ashraf starts a chicken business with fifty rupees. His wife hates Patna and frequently returns to her mother's house in Calcutta.

Late 1990—Shabnam is born.

Early 1993—Ashraf's son is born. A few months later he separates from his wife and leaves for Bombay.

1995—Ashraf leaves for Delhi and loses contact with his family back home.

1998—He returns to Bombay but is unable to find any of his friends and so leaves almost immediately for Surat, Gujarat.

1999—Works as a mazdoor in Surat, but hates it.

2000—Arrives in Delhi.

2007—Leaves for Calcutta.

'That's it, Aman bhai. Now you know everything about me—sab kuch. Like a government form: name, date of birth, mother's name, place of residence, everything. Our faces are pasted in your notebook, our voices all locked in your recorder—me, Lalloo, Rehaan, Kaka, J.P. Pagal, everyone. Now you know everything. What will we talk about if we ever meet again?'

We sit looking out of the first-floor balcony of the TB hospital in Calcutta. It's late evening; around us, wards burst into light as orderlies move floor by floor through the building, snapping on the lights as they go along.

'The past is done, Aman bhai. In future we will only talk about the future.'

EPILOGUE

If it's a missed call at six, it must be Ashraf. I have a list of numbers that make up the Cartesian coordinates of Ashraf's life in Calcutta: Ashraf Mustafa Bed 31 for when he's in his ward, Ashraf Paanwallah for when he steps out of the hospital compound for his evening walk, Ashraf Dost for the one time he ran away and got drunk. 'This is a friend of Ashraf's,' said a nervous voice on the telephone. 'You need to convince him to go back to the hospital.'

Soon after he returned to the hospital Ashraf moved to a new ward from where he called me every other day for three months. 'We have a TV here,' he said excitedly.

I told him I had moved into a new apartment. 'How much rent are you paying?' he asked.

Then Ashraf was told he would be discharged, 'around November last week', and I found myself a new job. 'You should be earning more with your degree from America,' he admonished.

The calls gathered frequency as the date of his discharge drew near. He spoke of setting up his vegetable business. I said I would arrange the money.

One evening in October, my phone rings at work.

'Sethi! It's me. I'm waiting in the rain, but your friend hasn't shown up.' It's Prithvi, one of my oldest and closest friends from Delhi. Prithvi moved to Calcutta last year and has since been helping out with Ashraf.

The previous month, I had pleaded with him to visit Ashraf and see if he was okay. 'I'll go to an MDR TB ward, Sethi,' he said manfully. 'Just don't ask me to do this again.'

Today he finds himself waiting in a downpour for Mohammed Ashraf to show up and take the five thousand rupees I had promised him on his discharge from the hospital. As a banker he is surprised at being kept waiting by someone who wants to borrow money. Creditors keep debtors waiting—not the other way around.

'Should I leave or stay?'

'Give him another ten minutes, no, Prithvi? Please?'

He calls back an hour later. 'Ashraf's taken the money,' he says. 'He says he'll call you.'

That was six months ago. Since then I have been fielding calls from his friends.

Mustafa called first. 'I can't find Ashraf. He got drunk and groped my landlord's daughter! So the landlord threw us out. I moved to my brother's house, but Ashraf just ran down the street with the whole mohalla giving chase and I haven't seen him since.'

'You know how he is, Aman bhai,' said Mustafa in a subsequent conversation when I called. 'I heard he has taken up a house near the airport. Some people went looking but they couldn't find him.'

'His tools are still with me. He hasn't come to collect them,' said Prabhu the bootlegger. 'Both Veeru and I miss him very much; he owes us a hundred rupees. This is how people repay kindness and gratitude.'

Mustafa still calls every few weeks; he hasn't given up. 'Any news, Aman bhai? I checked back at the hospital— nothing. I checked in Raja Bazaar; they haven't heard from him either.'

I tell him not to worry. Ashraf has my number, I've written it on every piece of paper in his sling bag. I've given him my visiting card. I've left my number with Dr Bannerjee at the hospital; Prabhu has it saved on his phone. Ashraf will find us when he wants to.

He'll probably call at two in the morning, his voice thick with whisky and laughter.

'Aman bhai,' he'll say. 'I hope I didn't disturb you. You should come see me sometime.'

A NOTE ON LANGUAGE

It is hard to offer an accurate glossary of the slang spoken on Delhi's streets, particularly since it is drawn from dialects all across north India and the same word carries multiple, context-specific connotations that are opaque to unfamiliar users. *Bhai*, for instance, is an honorific indicating "brother," a term of familiarity to describe social parity—though it can be a diminutive if used to indicate excessive familiarity with a social superior. *Bhaiyya* means "brother" as well and is subject to the same rules, but it is also used as a pejorative in Mumbai to describe working-class immigrants from Uttar Pradesh. Equals address one another with *beedu*.

The city's slang is coarse, vivid, and strewn with expletives. "Dialogue-*bazi*" is the favorite sport of the *Dilliwallah*, or Delhi denizen; *bazi* is the Urdu word for "sport," so dialogue-*bazi* is to speak in dialogue, like from a film. *Patang-bazi* is to fly a *patang*, or kite, and *laundi-bazi* is to play with a *laundi*, or young woman, and could imply anything from sex to romance to eve-teasing (that is, catcalling).

A Note on Language

If you were living the *mazdoor ki zindagi*, or laborer's life, in Delhi, you would spend your free time smoking *beedis*, or hand-rolled cheroots; drinking *desi sharab*, or country liquor; and eating *paneer*, or cottage cheese, at the *mandi*, or marketplace. But then, if you are reading this book, you are probably an *angrezi murgi*, or white hen. *Angrez* was originally used to describe the English, but is now a stand-in for generic "white person." When Rehaan and I first met, he called me an *angrezi murgi* to stress the distance between us. Gradually he started calling me *Bhai*, but never came around to calling me *Yaar*.

You must be careful when you speak with a *Bhai*, but a *Yaar* is the sort of close friend you can call a *Bhenchod*, or a sister fucker, in a fit of exasperation. Because unlike the other *chootiyas*, or pussies, you encounter on the streets of Delhi, a *Bhenchod* knows that we are all basically *haramis*, bastards, who work like *gulaams*, slaves, during the day, smoke a *chillum* of weed at night, and dream of *laundiyas*.

When dreaming of *laundiyas*, you could do worse than fantasizing about Aishwariya and Sushmita, those two *chamak challos* with their swinging hips who became Miss World and Miss Universe way back in 1994 but are still so hot that even a *gaandu*, an ass-fucker (pejorative for homosexual), would know who they are. *Chamak challos* are special—they aren't *randis*, or whores; they are the sort of girls who are coy enough, yet wise enough, to drop the *pallu* of their *sari* just enough to reveal a shapely bosom clad in a racy blouse that makes a man's heart race *chaka-chak chaka-chak chaka-chak* like the train from Patna to Calcutta.

Back home, every *basti*, or neighborhood, has its *chamak challos*, but in Delhi we are all *ajnabis*, or strangers. Some *mazdoors* are seasonal workers—*barsati mendaks*, rain frogs who come to the city for short visits between sowing and harvest—but for many, the *paanwallah*, who sells betel nut, *beedis*, and chewing tobacco, or *gutka*, is their first and closest friend. But how many close friends can the *paanwallah* have? For him, you are just another restless wastrel, a *lafunter*, who works when he can or simply shows up for *langar*, or free food, handed out by Sikh devotees after prayers at their *Gurudwara*, the Sikh place of worship.

It is true that the city is a hard place in which to live, but remember this isn't just any city. This is Delhi, where everyone is a *baazigar*, or gambler, and a man too timid to risk *kuch bhi*—anything—may lose *sab kuch*: everything.

ACKNOWLEDGEMENTS

This book would not have been possible without the extraordinary generosity and companionship of everyone at Bara Tooti Chowk, Sadar Bazaar. Lalloo, Rehaan, Sanjay Kumar (Kaka in the book), Munna, Lambu, Satish, Kalyani, J.P. Singh, and Bhagwan Das not only tolerated my persistent and intrusive presence, but made me a part of their lives and quests in the city. I am grateful for their patience with a lafunter like me.

I first began working on this manuscript on the suggestion of Aarti Sethi and Shuddhabrata Sengupta who read all my articles, essays, and drafts on Bara Tooti. Their intelligent and close reading of my manuscript kept me honest as a writer. Jeebesh Bagchi profoundly influenced my understanding spaces like Bara Tooti, and helped me think through ways of seeing, perceiving, and writing about Ashraf and his friends.

Rana Dasgupta read through the final proofs, smoothening

out sentences and gently disentangling mixed metaphors. I thank him for his incredible generosity.

I thank Bhrigupati Singh for wading through my early drafts and helping vary the pace of the narrative. Prithvi Chachra helped me out in Calcutta and visited Ashraf as he struggled with his illness. I also thank Akshaya and Ishan Tankha, Shiva Bajpai, Shovan Gandhi, Tushar Bajaj, and Anirvan Sen for their deep friendship and constant support through the years.

This book began as a project for the Sarai CSDS Independent Research Fellowship programme. I am grateful to everyone at Sarai for their generosity and camaraderie.

Chiki Sarkar's tireless editing has made this a much better book than I could have hoped to write.

I am indebted to Mohammed Ashraf, his stories, jokes, admonishments, and reminiscences. Thank you, Ashraf bhai.

A NOTE ON THE AUTHOR

Aman Sethi was born in Bombay in 1983. He studied chemistry in Delhi, and journalism in Chennai and New York. He is currently the Chhattisgarh correspondent for *The Hindu*. This is his first book.